George Heathcote

A Letter to the Right Honourable the Lord Mayor

the worshipful aldermen, and common-council; the merchants, citizens,

and inhabitants, of the city of London

George Heathcote

A Letter to the Right Honourable the Lord Mayor
the worshipful aldermen, and common-council; the merchants, citizens, and inhabitants, of the city of London

ISBN/EAN: 9783337195830

Printed in Europe, USA, Canada, Australia, Japan

Cover: Foto ©ninafisch / pixelio.de

More available books at **www.hansebooks.com**

To the RIGHT HONOURABLE The

LORD MAYOR,

The Worshipful ALDERMEN, and COMMON-COUNCIL;

THE

MERCHANTS, CITIZENS, and INHABITANTS,

OF THE

CITY of *LONDON*.

From an OLD SERVANT.

The THIRD EDITION.

Vox Populi, Vox Dei.

LONDON:

Printed for W. NICOLL, at the Paper-Mill, in St. Paul's Church-Yard. MDCCLXII.

[Price One Shilling and Six-pence.]

A LETTER

TO THE

Right Honourable the LORD MAYOR, &c.

My LORD *and* SIRS,

GRATITUDE, for the many great Favours and Honours you have formerly conferred upon me, will never permit my *Love* for the City of *London*, or my *Anxiety* for her *Interest* and Felicity, to cease or abate. And I can with Truth assure my good and worthy old Friends and Masters, that the Zeal, which, in the vigour of my life, warmed my Breast, for the Prosperity of my Fellow-Citizens, and of all my Fellow-Subjects, glows with no less Ardour, now I am old and grey-headed; and in the last Stage of my Journey to the other World.

This Zeal then, my Lord and Sirs, is my *sole* Motive, for addressing you, at this most important and critical Juncture; when, if any Credit is to be given to the publick Reports, all the Blessings, this Nation flattered itself with the Enjoyment of, from the Ruin of the *French* Commerce and naval Power, are in Danger of being lost, by the Restitution of *Goree* and *Guadaloupe*; if not of far the greatest Part of our late Conquests, to our perfidious and inveterate Enemy; and by leaving the *Newfoundland* Fishery, upon the Footing it stood before the War; which is not a Whit better, than giving them up that very profitable Branch of Trade and great Nursery of Seamen : The Profits annually arising from the Fish-Trade, together with those arising from *Guadaloupe* and *Goree*, being sufficient, with such a Nursery, to turn the Ballance of Trade in Favour of *France*; and revive their now expiring naval Force to an Height, that will enable her, in a few Years, to cope again with *Great Britain*, for the Dominion of the Sea ; and to insult, annoy, and injure *us*, and all her Neighbours.

These, my Lord and Sirs, must be certain Consequences of so dishonourable and shameful a Peace, as, the News Papers inform the Publick, is on the Anvil; and so far advanced, as to want little more to conclude it, than the Hands of the Duke *de Nivernois*, the *French* Ambassador, in *London*, and of our Minister in *Paris*. An Embassy honourable and safe to *Nivernois*: Honourable, because he comes to retrieve the lost Affairs of his royal Master, and the ruined Commerce and naval Power of his unfortunate Country ; by cajoling and outwitting (perhaps no arduous Undertaking) the *British* Ministry. He has no rich Sugar Plantations in the *West Indies* ; no *Goree* in *Africa*, a Settlement to carry on the Negro, the Ivory, the Gold Dust, and Gum Trades; no profitable Fishery and Nursery for Seamen ; no Colony in *North America* of Consequence enough to purchase a disadvantageous Peace of *Great Britain* ; standing, victorious and triumphant, over her often routed Enemy ; depressed and ruined beyond all Recovery ; without the friendly Aid of a *British* M————ry :—an Enemy now sprawling, trembling, languishing, and gasping under our Feet ; unable to lift either Hand or Heel against us. So that he, having nothing to give up of Value, *can* loose no Honour by betraying his Country. The very Attempt to bubble our Ministers, the Success of which must appear to all *Frenchmen*, so highly *improbable* and *romantick*, manifests

fests a Spirit, that of itself reflects great Honour upon the Ambassador, though he should return to his own Court *re infecta*.

But, my Lord and Sirs, if *Nivernois*, contrary to the reasonable Expectations of his Countrymen, should return to *France*, with the certain Means in his Pocket, of recovering so ample a Share of her late Commerce, as will turn the Ballance so much in her Favour, as will enable her to reimburse her squandered Wealth, retrieve her Bankrupt Credit, revive her naval Power, and fit out formidable Fleets; I say, if *Nivernois* should thus, by *Negotiation*, without spilling a Drop more of *French* Blood, be able to unravel and undo most, or so much of those glorious and unparallelled Services Mr. *Pitt* has done his Country; effected, by the Effusion of Oceans of *British* Blood, and the Expence of upwards of 100,000,000*l.* of Treasure, during the last and the present War; as will of Course draw after them all the Rest of the noble Acquisitions and glorious Conquests of the *British* Arms; planned by the unequalled Genius of that true Patriot and uncorrupt Servant of his King and Country; whose Absence from the Cabinet, every honest *Briton* justly laments, (and, if the *News Papers* tell Truth, of the Peace in Agitation) our latest Posterity will rue. I say then, if *Nivernois* should return to *France*, with such a rich Present in his Pocket for his Master and Fellow-Subjects; what Honour, what Glory, will not attend his Embassy? With what excessive Love, with what exquisite Delight, with what extatic Joy and extravagant Transports will his despairing, disgraced, and undone Prince and Fellow-Subjects, receive and behold, this *pacific* Deliverer of his Country; who without formidable Fleets and Armies, only with the Breath of his Mouth, shall have dissipated like a Bubble floating upon Water, all the immense Advantages of our Patriot Minister's wise and glorious

Administration—and "* *of mighty Battles fought in vain,—the Price of so much Blood and Treasure?"* How will the *Streets* of *Paris* ring, and every *Village* of *France* echo, with loud Acclamations and reiterated Praises of the Man, that with so much Facility shall have rescued *France* out of our Hands, and with the Ruins of *Britain* laid a solid Foundation of his Country's future Prosperity? Will not such honourable Testimonies of national Gratitude, be the Reward of *Nivernois*, in the same Manner, as they lately were of our Patriot Minister, for the like Services done his Country, with respect to *France?*

And as his Embassy will be honourable, so likewise it will be safe. For not having *betrayed*, but *saved* his *King* and *Country*, he will be *sure* of enjoying his *Titles* and *Estate* as long as he lives; and, when God demands his Life, of drawing his last Breath upon his *Pillow*, and descending into his *Grave* with his *Head* upon his *Shoulders.*—Great Blessings indeed! *which* God forbid should be permitted to any *Native* of this Island, that shall *dare* advise his Majesty to conclude an *unsafe* and *dishonourable* Peace with *France*; let that *Native* be born in the SOUTH, or let him be born in the NORTH.

But, my Lord and Sirs, let us leave Generals, and come to Particulars; and consider the Peace talked of upon the Plans laid down in the *News Papers.*

We are first alarmed with only the Restoration of *Goree* and *Guadaloupe*, and with leaving the *Newfoundland* Fishery upon the same Footing it was before the War.

We are next alarmed with Restitutions and Concessions, that must make every *Briton*'s Hair stand upright on his Head; make him turn pale and shudder at the Gulph of utter Destruction presented to his View, and said to be prepared for him. For

* *Addison's Cato.*

in

in the *London Evening-Poſt*, from *Tueſday Auguſt* the 31ſt, to *Thurſday September* the 2d, we have the following diſmal Account of the preſent Negotiation, threatening (if true) inevitable Perdition to *Great Britain.*

" The *following* are *confidently* ſaid in the publick News Papers, to be the *true* Preliminaries to the *enſuing* PEACE :

" The *Engliſh* to have all *Canada*; the River *Miſſiſſippi* to be the Boundaries.

" The *French* to retain the Privilege of ſending as many *Ships* as they *pleaſe* to *North America*; in which *Trade* they *uſually* employed annually between 1200 and 1500 ſail.

" The *French* to enjoy the Fiſhery they had before the War; and to be *given* the *Iſland* of *Cape Sable* for *drying* their FISH.—Likewiſe to have a Fiſhery on the Banks of *Newfoundland*, with a *Settlement* on the *Weſt Side* of that *Iſland* for the Purpoſes of drying, *&c.*

" *Martinico, Guadalcupe, Marigalante,* and *St. Lucia* to be *reſtored* to the *French*; *Tobago,* and the reſt of the *neutral Iſlands* to be ceded to *Great Britain.*

" The *French* to have three Settlements in the *Eaſt Indies*; *Pondicherry* to be one of them.

" *Minorca* to be ceded to the *Engliſh*; and *Belleiſle* to the *French.*

" *Senegal* to remain with the *Engliſh*; and *Goree* to be *reſtored.*

" The *Havannah,* alſo, if *taken,* to be *reſtored* to the *Spaniards.*"

Such Preliminaries, would be ſo *inſtantaneouſly* ruinous, and *ſhamefully* diſhonourable, that I can never believe any Miniſter *bold* enough, to make ſo *wicked* a *Sacrifice* of his Country's Honour; her moſt valuable commercial Intereſts, and naval Strength and Glory; as well as of her Independency on *France*; ſince he *muſt* know, ſo unjuſtifiable a Meaſure, would not only be attended with the Loſs of his *Royal Maſter's*

Master's Confidence, "whose *Heart is intirely* British," but also draw down upon his Head, the *implacable* RESENTMENT and INDIGNATION of the *whole* KINGDOM; and the *heaviest* and *crushing* WEIGHT of *parliamentary* JUSTICE and VENGEANCE. I am therefore inclined to think, that this *black* Catalogue of Preliminaries has been sent to the *London Evening-Post*, by some Enemy of our *great Ones*; or, if by some Friend, or with their Privity, that it is inserted, only to feel the Pulse of the People, in order to discover, how far they would be passive, under a Scheme pregnant with the worst Misfortunes that can befal a Nation; in Hopes, that when they see a Scheme, whereby less is to be given up, and the consequent Ruin will be more obscured from Sight and slower in its Approach, though not less *certain*, they may in a Fit of Joy, for their imaginary Escape from the more visible, eagerly embrace the invisible Danger; or that Stomachs nauseating a large Potion, may be prevailed on to take down a small Vial, without thinking the smaller Dose may be compounded strong enough to kill, as well as the large one; and, by the Skill of the Artist, the Poison may be contrived to operate with slow, and yet sure Degrees.

Thus, my Lord and Sirs, whether the *Preliminaries* now in Agitation, are only for the Restitution of *Goree, Guadaloupe*, and permitting the *French* to fish as before the War; or whether they are for that *ample* and *general* Restitution given us in the *London Evening-Post* of the 31st Instant, which will, like Gunpowder, blow up this Nation in a Trice; it will be *proper* to reduce to Figures, *what* will be the State of *Great Britain* and *France*, under a Peace concluded upon such *unequal* and *pernicious* PRELIMINARIES.

But before we state this Account, it may not be improper to observe, that, whichsoever of the *two Nations*, shall possess a *Ballance* of *Trade* in her Favour,

vour, confisting in an Importation of foreign Coin or Bullion, and only possess a Right in that great Nursery of Seamen, must of Necessity become the most powerful, both in external and internal Strength; and that the weakest must fall a Victim to that State which shall thus become the superior. Strength and Power. And that consequently the future Security, Happiness, and Glory of *Great Britain* absolutely depends upon keeping that Balance of foreign Coin and Bullion, and the great Nursery of Seamen in our own hands: And that whoever shall, in making a Peace with *France*, make such Concessions to *her*, as shall turn that *Balance* and *restore* her *naval Power*, will infallibly raise the *Greatness* of *France*, out of the *Ruins* of *Britain*; unless the Parliament, in Compassion to a betrayed People, shall prevail with his M———y immediately to break so *unequal, pernicious*, and *unnecessary* a PEACE.

Mr. *John Ashley*, an Author of compleat Knowledge in all Branches of our Plantation and *North American* Trade; an Author of allowed Credit, whose Authority hath never been denied or disputed, tells us in his *Memoirs and Considerations*, &c. printed 1740.

"That it is computed, there is the Quantity of about 80,000 *English* Hogsheads of Sugar imported into *Germany, Holland,* the *Baltick, Spain, Italy,* and *Turkey, per Annum,* (exclusive of what is imported into *Holland* and *Spain* from their own Plantations) which Quantity may employ 40,000 Tons of Shipping, and 3600 Seamen, *only* to bring it into *Europe*; and amounts in Value to 1,000,000*l*. Sterling *per Annum*, computing at 12*l*. 10*s. per* Hogshead, Freight and Commissions included. *"

Note, Besides 40,000 Tons of Shipping and 3600 Seamen employed, in only the Importation into *Europe* of 80,000 *English* Hogsheads of Sugar from the

Sugar

* See *Ashley*'s Memoirs and Considerations, p. 19 and 20.

Sugar Islands, at 12*l.* 10*s. per* Hogsheads, amounts to 1,000,000*l.* Sterling *per Annum,* exclusive of Indigo, Ginger, Cotton, and Coffee, &c. which must be a vast Sum; and which 1,000,000*l.* they cost the Merchants (not the Mother Countries, for they buy them with Manufactures) that export them again to the several *European* Markets. This 1,000,000*l.* before the *Re-exportation,* indeed brings in no foreign Coin or Bullion into the Mother Countries; but is nevertheless of prodigious Advantage to them, by giving *Bread* to vast Numbers of *People.* To 3600 Seamen employed in the first Importation of those Sugars into *Europe,* and to the Seamen employed in the Re-exportation of them to the *European* Markets; which may be as many more.——To all the several Artificers employed in building and fitting out those 40,000 Tons of Shipping.——To the Manufacturers almost of all Sorts, who supply the Seamen and Artificers, their Wives and Children, with Rayment of every Kind, and Houshold Goods; and also to those Manufacturers, who make wearing Apparel fit for the Natives of *Africa,* and Trinkets and Baubles, with which the Mother Countries buy Negroes to cultivate both their Sugar Islands and Colonies in *North America,* and to the Husbandman who raises Provisions to feed all these useful People. Besides, they purchase with those Manufactures as much Gum, as perhaps would cost, were they to be purchased of Foreigners, 100,000*l.* Sterling *per Annum*; a very great Saving. And over and above all this, they purchase, with those Manufactures, great Quantities of *Gold Dust* to coin into Specie, Elephants Teeth and Negroes, sold to *New Spain*; where they have an Opportunity, at the same Time, of vending large Quantities of their Manufactures, for both which last they have their Returns in Silver, to coin also into Specie. So that, by Manufactures alone, without exporting

a Brass

a Brafs Farthing, they supply and cultivate their Sugar Islands and Northern Colonies with Negroes, save the Price of Gums, and annually encrease in Wealth, by the Importation of Gold Dust from *Africa*, the Sale of Negroes, and dry Goods in *New Spain*, and the Profits upon 80,000 Hogsheads of Sugar, valued at Home at 1,000,000l. Sterling *per Annum*; besides what they gain by Cotton, Ginger, Indigo, and Coffee. So that by Means of their Sugar Islands and Settlements in *Africa* having a vast Demand for Manufactures, whereby they plentifully maintain their Poor, and whereby they are invited to marry; and Foreigners that cannot live at Home, are induced to flock to them, to gain Subsistance by Labour; in so much that the Number of People encreases proportionably with their Wealth. And thus, both external and internal Strength encreasing daily, they are enabled to raise great Armies and formidable Fleets. And all these great Advantages lately (except a very poor Pittance) were engrossed by *France*.

Now, my Lord and Sirs, let us ask our great Statesmen the following Questions; to which Truth would dictate to them the annexed Answers:

Q. 1: Which, before the War, were the Mother Countries of those valuable Sugar Islands and Settlements, from whence all this immense Wealth ariseth?

A. Great Britain and *France*.

Q. 2. Of the 80,000 Hogsheads *English* Weight, how many did *Great Britain* export to *Germany*, *Holland*, the *Baltick*, *Spain*, *Italy*, and *Turkey*, upon an Average *communibus Annis*, from 1733 to 1736; and how many from the Year 1736 to 1737?

A. According to Mr *Ashley's* Account from the Year 1733 to 1736, the Exportation is:

To *Germany*, and the other Markets of *Europe*, Raw Sugars, Hogsheads — } 1155 *per An.*
To *Ireland*, Ditto — 4602 Ditto
To *British* Plantations, *Alderney*, *Guernsey*, *Jersey*, *Africa*, and the *East Indies*, Ditto — } 25 Ditto

Total of raw Sugars — — 5782 *per An.*
To *Germany*, &c. refined Sugars exported from 1729 to 1736, Hogsheads — — } 1118
To *Ireland* — — 381
To *British* Plantations, &c. as above 494

Total of refined Sugars — 1993

Total of raw and refined Sugars — 6875

From 1736 to 1737 the Demand from *Germany* and the other foreign Markets funk greatly, for we exported raw Sugars to them only, Hogsheads 258
To *Ireland* — — — 3740
To the *British* Plantations, &c. — 80

4078
To *Germany*, &c. of refined Sugars 168
To *Ireland* — — 581
To *British* Plantations, &c. — 384--1133

Total of raw and refined Sugars — 5211
See *Memoirs and Considerations*, p. 96 and 97.

And thus the Demand for the *British* Sugars, between the Years 1715 and 1719 to 1736, has annually declined; 'till the Exportation funk from 19,202 Hogsheads, inclusive of 622 Hogsheads of refined Sugar *per Annum* from 1715 to 1736, to 5211 Hogsheads,

heads, and continued still sinking, till the Exportation fell to little more than half that Number, when Almighty God was pleased to bless the *national* Fleets and Armies in *America* with astonishing Success against our Enemy, in the present War.

Q. Who supplied the foreign Markets with the remaining 74,789 Hogsheads?

A. France did before the War, *Great Britain* since; for *Spain* and *Holland* do not raise Sugars enough for their own Consumption, therefore they cannot supply any foreign Market.

Q. Where does *France* raise that large Quantity of Sugars sufficient to serve all *Europe*, over and above her own Consumption?

A. From *Martinico, Guadaloupe, Marigalante,* and *St. Lucia,* and her Part of *Hispaniola.*

Q. As we have taken all these rich Sugar Plantations from *France*, except the last, at a very great Expence, why will you restore to *France* Places, from whence she drew such immense Riches, as enabled her to reduce your *native* Country to extreme *Despair* and the Brink of Ruin; and thereby restore your faithless and inveterate Enemy to that tremendous Strength and Magnitude, by Sea and Land; the Consequences of which lately so much alarmed *Great Britain?*

A. France will not make Peace with us if we do not give up all these with *Goree*; without which, she cannot have Negroes, and many other valuable Branches of Trade; nor without we give her also the Fishery for a Nursery for Seamen, whom the Sale of the Fish caught will pay.

Q. Are you induced tamely to surrender most of the Advantages of the War, because you have not Talents to conduct a War? or because you think we cannot bear the profuse Expences of a continental War, useless and ruinous to *Britain*; and that *France* will not let us have a Peace in *Germany*; without which H——r cannot be safe, if we act a wise Part, and recal Home our Troops? Or do both these Reasons co-operate?

A. Hum—Hum—Hum.

Q. Do you not know, if you advise your Master to make an unsafe and dishonourable Peace, tending to raise *France* again from her present low Condition, to her late dangerous Prosperity, which had almost undone *Great Britain,* and threatened her and all the States of *Europe* with *French* Slavery, under universal Monarchy; do you not know, I say, that the People are in Possession of an undoubted Right, as antient as the Entrance of the *Saxons,* and confirmed a-fresh to them at the Revolution by the Bill of Rights, to lay their Grievances before the Throne, and to petition for Redress, and for the Removal of evil Councellors? And do you not know likewise, that the People have a Right to lay their Grievances before their Representatives assembled in Parliament, and petition them to bring Ministers to the Bar of Justice, for Misbehaviour in Administration; and that the Commons of *Great Britain* can, in Parliament assembled, impeach Ministers; and that if they are proved guilty, the Lords can inflict Punishments adequate to their Crimes; and that the two Houses of a *British* Parliament can with the Royal Assent (if necessary or expedient) *confiscate Estates,* and *condemn* to the Scaffold or Gibbet, even by a Law *ex post facto?* What Reason then have you to imagine, that *all these* will not exercise their several Rights, and discharge the Duties they owe the Community they are Members of, whenever the very Existence of their Country is at Stake; and the Preservation of it depends, upon an *Exaction* of the *severest* JUSTICE?

A. Oh Mercy! Mercy! Mercy!

To such an Answer the People would be (I believe) very apt to reply, JUSTICE—JUSTICE—JUSTICE—HEADS and CONFISCATIONS.

But, my Lord and Sirs, let us return to our Computations, which will evince the Folly and Danger of restoring any Thing to *France*, or making any Peace with her; at least, before we have driven, that all devouring wild Beast, out of every Part of *America*.

We have seen in the preceding Sheets, that the Plantations, *Goree*, and the Fishery are Springs, whence stream immense national Commerce, Riches, and Strength, both in internal and external; and that our perfidious, thieving, irreconcilable Enemy hath received the Benefits arising from them, superior to *Great Britain*, in a Degree most amazing, frightful, and alarming; a Degree that very lately threatened a *full Period* to the national Existence of this Island; and will, one Day or other, certainly put a *full* Period to it, if we cede or restore any one Thing to her in *America*, or *Africa*. The only Difference to us will be, that we shall sink into a *French* Province, and become *French* Slaves, sooner or later, according to the Number of Concessions we shall make, and Conquests we shall restore.

This will more clearly appear, from the following State of the Ballance of Trade between *Great Britain* and *France*, with respect to the Importation of Bullion and foreign Coin.

An Account of Bullion and foreign Coin imported into *Great Britain* and *France*, by Means of the *West India*, *North American*, and *African* Trades; on which I will remark, as I proceed.

The SUGAR PLANTATIONS.

Imported from the Plantations, only in raw Sugar for Exportation to the *European* Markets, —— Hogsheads 80,000, at 12*l*. 10*s. per* Hhd. 1,000,000*l*.

Whereof

Whereof *Great Britain* imported, at the Time Mr. *Ashley* published his Book, no more than 5211 Hogsheads; which we will subtract from the 80,000, and the Remainder were imported by the *French*.

Hogsheads of Sugar imported —— 80000
By *Great Britain*, Ditto —— —— 5211
Remainder imported by *France* —— 74789

Next let us see what these Sugars bring in, clear Profit, to each Nation in Bullion and foreign Coin; for, what we said before, respects only the Subsistance of their People, by the Manufactures, wherewith they purchase Negroes to cultivate their Colonies, and augment their internal, and, in some Degree, their external Strength, &c.

25*l per Cent*. is, I believe, a moderate Advance, on Sugars valued at 1,000,000*l*. when exported to foreign Markets; of which Sugars are exported

By *Great Britain* 5211 Hhds, at 12*l*. 10*s*. valued at home amounts to 65137*l*. sold at foreign Markets at 25*l. per Ct*. advance, which is so much Bullion, or foreign Coin brought into *Britain*, and is clear Gain to the Nation; if not to the Merchants,	£ 81422	Imported by *France* 74789 Hhds. at 12*l*. 10*s. per* Hhd. valued at Home, amounts to 934863 *l*. sold at foreign Markets at 25*l. per Cent*. profit, is a clear Gain to *France* of so much Bullion or foreign Coin brought into *France*,	£ 1,168,578
Balance in Bullion and foreign Coin in favour of *France* against *Great Britain per Annum*,	1,087,156		
	1,168,578		1,168,578

The Profit arising from Indigo, Ginger, Pimento Cotton, Coffee, &c. must be in Favour of *France* greatly, for these Reasons: Our Duties upon the Products of our Plantations are exorbitantly high; and Freight, Wages, and victualling Ships, so much dearer than they are in *France*, that she vends

not

not only her Sugars, but all the other Products of her Plantations, at least 25 *per Cent.* cheaper than *Great Britain* can; which is the Reason of our losing the foreign Markets, and of the late dangerous Encrease of the *French* Trade, and Growth of her late formidable naval Power. And these Misfortunes have been entirely owing to our impolitic interfering in *German* Quarrels and continental Connections, which we have been unfortunately drawn into by a Predilection for *H****r*, which one might hope is now at an End; when we have the Happiness to see a Prince on the Throne, who has assured us from it, *that his Heart is intirely* British. These unnational and ruinous Connections with the Continent, from whence *Great Britain* can reap no Advantage, have not only prevented us from discharging our *Plantations* and *northern Colonies* of those heavy Duties, and the Mother Countries of those heavy Taxes, which has given *France* the Means of serving the foreign Markets 25 *per Cent.* cheaper than *Britain* can, by paying off the national Debt of 46,000,000*l.* left by Queen *Anne*; but have encreased that Load of Debt to the monstrous Sum of about 130,000,000*l.* But to return to the Products of the *French* Plantations of Indigo, Ginger, *&c.*

What the exact Quantity of these several Products of the Plantations is, or what Value they bear in the Mother Countries; how much exported to foreign Markets, and what Prices they fetch there, I am not able to say. But surely, if we estimate them in foreign Markets at no more than One-fifth of the Sale of the *French* Sugars, we cannot greatly err.

France then we see sells her 74,789 Hhds of Sugar at foreign Markets for the Amount of £. 1,168,578
The fifth Part of which will be about   -   233,716

Total Sale in foreign Markets of Products   1,402,294

Great

Great Britain, we will say, sells the Quantity of the same Products in foreign Markets, in the same Proportion:

	£.
Her Vend of Sugars amounts to	81,422
The fifth Part of which is about	16,284
	97,706

Sale of Indigo, Ginger, &c. of *Great Britain* to foreign Markets, amounts to about — 16,284
The Sale of Ditto of *France* to about — 233,716

Total — — — £. 250,000

Upon this 250,000*l*. Profit to the Mother Countries on Indigo, Ginger, &c. how stands the Balance?

	£.		£.
Great Britain receives only	16,284	*France* receives	233,716
By Balance in favour of *France*,	217,432		
	233,716		233,716

Now let us see under one View, how the Ballance stands between *Great Britain* and *France*, upon all Products of the Sugar Plantations.

	£.		£.
Great Britain received for 5211 Hhds of Sugars, from foreign Markets,	81,422	*France* received for 74789 Hhds of Sugars from foreign Markets	1,168,578
For Indigo, Ginger, and other Products,	16,284	For Indigo, Ginger, &c.	233,716
Total	97,706	Total	1,402,294
Balance on the Plantations in Favour of *France*,	1,304,588		

North America next presents itself to our Consideration. This Trade, perhaps, hath been our main Support, under the last and present *French* Wars; and

and our various *Don Quixote*-Enterprizes upon the Continent, attended with immense, profuse, and extravagant Subsidies; paid in their Turns, just as the mutable Politics of ambitious *H****r* required, not only to all the great and respectable Princes and Powers of *Europe*, but to the little *insignificant* Princes of *Germany*, (I think they call them *Princes*) those *mere* Shadows—those feint Resemblances and farcical Mimics of potent, absolute Monarchs—*little insignificant Princes*, indeed! in all whose *Territories united*, never since the World stood forth, passed so much *Gold* and *Silver*, as since 1714, hath been conveyed into the *most inconsiderable* of all those *inconsiderable* Principalities.——Principalities, indigent to a Degree, that no longer ago than Queen *Anne*'s Reign, if in the Richest of them, so small a Sum of Money, as the Amount of 5000*l*. Sterling is, could by any Means have been collected and amassed into one Heap, it is scarce a Question, that Curiosity, natural to the lower Class to see raree Shows, would have drawn from the remotest Confines of the *narrow* Domain, all the *miserable* Slaves of the *petty Despotic*, to behold a Novelty, which had never blessed the Eye-sight of their Fore-fathers; and which, in those Days, they themselves could never have hoped to see again. And I heartily pray *God*, that a *single* Guinea may not, by the Expiration of the present *Century*, if we make *Peace* with *France* upon the most *plausible* Plan talked of, be as great a Novelty, and afford as much Wonder and Transport in this Island.

The Trade of *North America*, I say, hath been, perhaps, under all our late Difficulties and Dangers, our *main* Support. For, from whence could we have been supported, except from our Northern Colonies? The *European* Markets for *European* Goods, since *France* by the Cheapness of Labour and partly by procuring the *English* and *Irish* Wool, had got so

D   large

large a Share of them before the War, that if we went Halves with her, perhaps it was as much as we did, would hardly have defrayed the exorbitant Charges of the afore-mentioned un-national Meaures.

The *East India* Trade, of which *France* had also a great Share, we all muſt know would have been inſufficient for the Purpoſe. As to our Sugar Iſlands: The above given State of their Products and Profits clearly demonſtrates their total Inability, to have yielded the leaſt Support to their Mother Country.——For the Fleets and Armies neceſſary to defend her from the over-growing and menacing Power of *France*, as well as thoſe numerous Land *Forces*, ſent, to manure with *Britiſh* Blood and *mangled* Corpſes, the ſterile Plains of *Germany*, could not be maintained, without freſh and plentiful annual Imports of *Bullion*; to reimburſe the *Millions* laviſhed upon the *aggrandizing* of *H****r*, and *neceſſarily* expended in Defence of our *commercial* Rights in *French* and *German* Wars; of which the *Partiality* of former *Miniſters* towards that Electorate, has been the primary and ſole Cauſe. For how could 5211 Hogſheads of Sugars, raw and refined, which is all our Exportation in 1737, incluſive of *Ireland*, (and the Exportation ſunk lower, I think, afterwards) poſſibly return ſufficient Profits, to pay ſuch Fleets and Land Armies; and to reimburſe the Nation, for thoſe exorbitant and *unjuſtifiable* Sums of *Specie*, exported to *Germany* for the Benefit of *H****r*. All the *Service* therefore our Sugar Plantations have lately been of to the *Mother* Country, has been to ſave her the Coſt of her own Conſumption; to ſupply *Ireland*, and employ the Poor, as far as the joint Conſumption of *Britain* and *Ireland* would go, in encouraging our Manufactures.

Had this unhappy Nation been bleſſed, for this laſt 50 Years, with *honeſt* and *wiſe* Miniſters, our Sugar Plantations would have been of that *extenſive* Profit and

and Advantage to us, which those of *France* have been to her.

This *Inability*, therefore, to succour the *Mother Country* farther than I have observed, is not owing to any *Deficiency* in the Products of our Plantations, but to a *Deficiency* in the *Abilities* and *Honesty* of our M——rs; who, for continental Interests, have neglected to pay off the publick Debt, and take off the heavy Duties upon those Products; thereby enabling the *French* (who have been very careful to encourage their Settlements) to undersel us in the foreign Markets. And happy, thrice happy is it for us, though our Northern Colonies have not been less taxed, nor better treated, than the Sugar Islands, that *France* hath not had Time yet to people and cultivate their Northern Colonies, sufficiently to interfere with the Products of ours. If they had the Products of our Northern Colonies, would have gone to Market under the like Disadvantages with our Sugars, and have been of no more Benefit to us in our Distress.

A State of the Products of our Northern Colonies, and the Profits of Bullion and foreign Coin.

Virginia *and* Maryland.

Tobacco imported into *Great Britain* annually upon the Average——Hogsheads 65,000, Value here at 15*l. per* Hogshead £. 975,000

Home Consumption about 20,000 Hhds.

	£.
Remainder exported—Hogsheads 45,000	675,000
Advance on the said at 25 *per Cent.*	168,750
Total Profit on exported Tobacco — —	843,750

Carolina.

CAROLINA.

Mr. *Ashley*, in his *Memoirs and Considerations*, assures us, that *Carolina*, in a good Year, will produce 80,000 Barrels of Rice of 4 Cwt. *per* Barrel; and upon a Medium of seven Years, makes 50,000 Barrels *per Annum*; that 2000 Barrels are *consumed in* Great Britain *and* Ireland, *p.* 18. Rice imported into *Great Britain*, Barrels 50,000 Value Sterling annually to *Great Britain* 80,000*l.* as Mr. *Ashley* says this, after mentioning 48,000 Barrels exported, *that* 80,000*l.* I suppose, is the Principal and Profit of the 50,000 Barrels; so will only value it -- -- } *£.* 80000

New England, *New York*, *Pensylvania* are mighty Benefactors to *Great Britain* in the Consumption of her Manufactures of Apparel, for the Inhabitants of these Provinces, and their Negroes, and almost of every other Kind of Manufactures; besides the great Quantities of them vended upon the Coast of *Africa*, for the Purchase of Negroes. But they do not confine their Blessings here: Their Products imported are extremely useful, and absolutely necessary, both in our Shipping and Manufactures; such as we cannot be without, and must therefore buy them of other Countries, and chiefly with our Money; since we must have them from Places, that will take little or nothing of us, but our Money: As *France* and the Northern Countries, who, though they must have warm Cloathing, will certainly prefer the *French* Market, where they can be furnished much cheaper than by *Great Britain*; whose *Specie* thus goes out to pay for the necessary Raiment of the *Northern* Countries. So that if these Provinces were of no other Advantage than employing our Poor, and saving the national Specie, these alone would be very great.

And

And, with Respect to the last, let us remember the old *Adage*, " a **Penny** saved is a *Penny* got." But some of our Manufactures, worked up with these Materials, may perhaps find foreign Markets; and such of them that do, certainly bring in Bullion.

Whatever Benefits may arise from these Products, as the Exports may be very few, and not knowing the exact Quantity, we cannot carry them to the Account of Importation of Bullion and foreign Coin; and, indeed, 'tis *unnecessary*, as the *French Northern* Colonies are to *France*, as yet of no other Benefit than ours are to us, and indeed scarce so much. But if she is permitted to retain any Part of *North America*, there can be no Doubt she will try at *Tobacco Rice*, and *whatever* else of our Settlements, introduce *Bullion* to the *Mother* Country. *Virginia* and *Maryland* may then spare the far greatest Part of their Care and Industry, in the Cultivation of their Lands. For the Product of *Tobacco*, being so *heavily taxed* here; and *France* being thereby enabled to carry that *Commodity* as much *cheaper* than *Great Britain*, as they *now* do their *Sugars*, the Demand for the *Tobacco* of *Virginia* and *Maryland* will, *like* that of the *Sugars* of our *Plantations*, be reduced to the *Consumption* of their *Mother* Country, and *Ireland*; which is much the same Thing; and we shall loose that Fountain, whence we now draw such Stores of Bullion and foreign Coin.

Hudson's Bay is certainly a very profitable and rich Trade; but being in few Hands, of a very small Company of Merchants, who keep the Profits, as much as possible, a Secret among themselves, an exact Discovery of the national Advantages accruing from it, may not, perhaps, be so easily made. However, we may be satisfied, they are very considerable; but yet not so exceeding great, but that they may be balanced, or even exceeded by the *French* Trade in the same Commodities, with which the *Indians* supply

ply it; and which are brought down the *Mississipi* into the Gulph of *Mexico*, to be brought to *Europe*.

Newfoundland Fishery is the last Consideration, with respect to *North America*; a weighty and important Consideration indeed! I shall here, my good old Friends and Masters, trouble you with few more Observations, than are absolutely necessary, from the Nature of so momentous a Concern; having annexed to this Letter, a Transcript from the *British-Merchant*, which will convey to such of my Fellow-Citizens, whose Trades and Occupations may not *directly* lead them to Enquiries of this Kind; though every Individual must, in some Degree, more or less, be concerned in this Subject; the fatal Consequences inevitable, of permitting *France*, or any Nation, the Enjoyment of any Privilege or Liberty in those Seas.

The Objects then of our present Consideration are two, *viz.*

The Profits arising from the *Newfoundland* Fishery, with respect to the Importation of Bullion and foreign Coin into *Great Britain*.

The support and Augmentation of that naval Power, that shall enjoy them.

And first for the first of these. The Profits arising from the *Newfoundland* Fishery; these are annually very great, Mr. *Ashley* says, p. 18 and 19 of his *Memoirs and Considerations*, &c. that from *Newfoundland*, *New England*, and *Nova Scotia*, there are about 300 Sail of Ships, great and small; or about 30000 Tons of Shipping employed annually in carrying Fish to *Portugal, Spain*, and *Italy*; which employ about 2700 Seamen; and may, by a Circulation in Trade, return to *Great Britain* about 260,000*l*. Sterling *per annum* in this Article of Fish; besides Train-Oil, and Whalebone; of which there may be imported into *Great Britain* to the Value of 40000*l*. annually and upwards: and it is computed, that about two Thirds of all these Advantages arise from the Fishery of *Newfoundland* only.

only. How much of this Train-Oil and Whale-bone may be re-exported, I cannot say. But it is plain, from Mr. *Ashley*'s Account, that 260,000*l*. Sterling is annually brought into *Great-Britain*, from the Article of Fish alone. Let us suppose then, that so much of the Train-Oil and Whale-bone is exported, either in manufactured or unmanufactured Goods, as will bring in the above Value of 40,000*l*. Sterling into *Great Britain*. Then the whole Sum of 300,000*l*. would be returned to *Great Britain* in Bullion.——This then is allowing the utmost Profit to this Nation upon the Fishery.

In the Preliminaries herein early mentioned, that give *France* a Right to send as many Ships as she pleases to *North America*, an Observation is thrown in, and I believe it to be true, that she usually employed annually from 1200 to 1500 Ships in that Trade. I am informed, that the Number of Ships employed to *Canada* and the other *French* Settlements which lye behind ours, seldom exceed Six; which are loaded with Fur-Trees, and Furs bought of the Indians; and all her other Trade upon the Continent of *America*. If these two Facts are true, as I am credibly informed they are, a most melancholy Prospect opens to the View of every honest *Briton*.——A Prospect of nothing better than a total Annihilation of the Naval Power of *Great Britain*, and her Reduction to the miserable Condition of a *French* Province. For, if she usually employed from 1200 to 1500 Ships in that Trade annually, there must be employed each Year, upon the Average, 1350; and if only six of them in her own Continent, the Remainder (*viz.*) 1344 could be employed no where but in the Fishery. Then *Great Britain* having employed no more than 300 Ships in that Fishery, and thereby gained no more than 300,000*l*. *per Annum*.——*France* that employed about four Times and a half as many Ships in that Trade, must have gained about four Times and a half

as

as much as *Great Britain*; that is, about 1,350,000*l.* for if 300 Ships give 300000, 1350 Ships being four Times and a half that Number, muſt give four Times and a half as much; unleſs the *French* Ships are of a different Size from ours. But the *French* are too wiſe to ſend ſmaller, and larger would turn the Scale more in their Favour. But let us ſee the Account of this pretty Preſent, that we are about to make *France*, with reſpect to the Ballance of Bullion.

State of the Ballance of Bullion Imported into the Mother Countries from the Newfoundland *Fiſhery*.

GREAT BRITAIN		FRANCE	
receives for Fiſh exported,	£ 300,000	receives for ditto	£ 1,350,000
		Ballance in Favour of *France*,	1,050,000

I proceed to the ſecond Object of our Conſideration, *viz.* The Support and Augmentation of that Naval Power that ſhall enjoy them.

And here we have a ſad Preſage of the inevitable Subverſion of our naval Power; and, conſequently, of our future Subjection to *French* Tyranny: For how will it be poſſible to elude the Yoke, when that Nation is become ſo greatly ſuperior to us, in Commerce, Riches, and naval Power, as *France* muſt neceſſarily be rendered, by permitting her to caſt her Nets and Lines in the Seas of *America*? A ſhort State of the different Number of Seamen employed in our Fiſhery and that of *France*, will at one View evince the Neceſſity of refuſing her this deſtructive Liberty.

But I ſhall firſt make the following Obſervation on Mr. *Aſhley*'s Calculation. That altho' he has ſet forth the Number of Ships and Men employed in carrying the *Fiſh* when catched and cured, to the *European* Markets; yet he has wholly omitted the Number of Ships and Men employed, firſt in catching and curing the ſaid Fiſh, and afterwards carrying home to the

Mother Countries, the Oil produced from the Liver of the Codfish, and the Men employed in the Fishery.

I shall make no Addition to his Number of Ships, altho' that would be very considerable; but in order to open a View to my Country of that great Nursery of Seamen, the Source of her Naval Strength and Power, and which will give the Sovereignty of the Sea to such Nation as shall become possessed of the same, it will be absolutely necessary for me to bring into this Computation the Number of Men employed in it.

There are two Fisheries for Codfish belonging to *Newfoundland*; one is called the Bank, the other the Shore Fishery. The first is Fish catched in Ships on the Banks of *Newfoundland*, and is therefore called Bank Fish; the last is Fish catched in open Boats on Shoals or Ledges near the Shore, and for that Reason is called Shore Fish. To this last I shall confine myself, as in no Respect, it interferes with Mr. *Ashley*'s Computation, and will sufficiently shew the vast Importance of the *Newfoundland* Fishery: altho' if the Men employed in the *Newfoundland*, *New England* and *Nova Scotia* Bank Fisheries were to be enumerated, they would, no doubt of it, greatly inlarge the Account.

Before the last War, *England* had no less than 1000 Boats annually employed in the Shore Fishery of *Newfoundland*, from *Fogoa* round to *Placentia* and St. *Peter*'s. To each Boat is generally allowed 4 Fishermen and 2 Shore men: Then by this Computation, the Number of Men employed, before the last War, in the *English Newfoundland* shore Fishery only, amounted annually to 6000, which added to the 2700 computed by Mr. *Ashley*, makes 8700 Men annually employed.

The *French*, by Mr. *Ashley*'s Calculation, having four times and a half as many Ships and Men employed in carrying their Fish to Market, as the *English* had, one would imagine they should have four times

and

and a half as many more Men employed in Catching, and Curing their Fish; but as their Mud-Fish does not require as many hands to Cure it as the Baccaloa, I shall suppose them to have had only three Times the quantity employed in the Shore Fishery the *English* had, *Viz.* 3000 Boats and 18000 Men, which being added to 12096 Seamen, Mr. *Ashley*'s Computation, makes 30096 Men annually employed by *France* in her *American* Fisheries before the last War, and that both Nations employed annually 38866 Men, every one of which being so much used to the Sea as to be made on his first Entrance on board a Man of War an useful Seaman; and of this great Number *France* annually employed 21396 Men more than *England* did. This Calculation is so moderate that no other Exception can be made to it, but its being much below the Mark, and in Fact what it really should be.

A State of the Number of British *and* French *Ships and Seamen employed in the Fishery.*

Great Britain employed in the Newfoundland Fishery.		France employed in the Newfoundland Fishery.	
Ships	Seamen, &c.	Ships	Seamen
300	8700	1344	30,096
Balance 1,044	21,396	300	8700
1,344	30,096	superior to Britain 1044	21,396

A State of the Number of Ships and Seamen employed by Great Britain *and* France, *upon the whole Trade to* North America.

	Great Britain employed,		France employed	
	Ships.	Seamen.	Ships.	Seamen.
In Tobacco	400	3600		
In Rice	100	600		
In Fishery	300	8700	In Fishery	1344	30,096
In the rest of the Colonies,	300	2700	In the rest of their Colonies,	6	54
Total	1100	15,000	Total	1350	30,150
Balance	250	14,250	Deduct	1100	15,900
	1,350	30,150	Superior to *Britain*	250	14,250

Here

Here I beg it may be carefully observed, how vastly superior *France* appears to *Great Britain*, in Ships and Seamen, by this very Fishery alone; which furnisheth her with about 250 Ships, and about 14,250 Seamen more than our Share, and all our Northern Colonies together do *Great Britain*.

We will now, my Lord and Sirs, if you please, take a View of the naval Strength of *Great Britain* and *France*, arising from the Sugar Plantations.—— No agreeable Prospect,

Great Britain then, having, before the War, but about *one-fifteenth* Part of the 80,000 Hogsheads of Sugars imported into *Europe*, for Re-exportation to *Germany*, &c. she could employ in that Importation no more of the 400 Ships employed in it, than one-fifteenth Part; which is about 26 Ships : And, consequently, she could employ no more than one-fifteenth Part of the Seamen in it; which is about 240; So that, with respect to the Navigation from our Sugar Plantations, *France* hath a vast Superiority over *Great Britain*, in Ships and Seamen.

A State of Ships and Seamen of Great Britain *and* France.

	Ships.	Seamen.		Ships.	Seamen.
Great Britain employed	26	240	*France*	374	3360
				26	240
Remains to *France* superior to G. Britain				348	3120

The Trade to *Africa* was to *France*, before the War, very considerable, in Point of Bullion; and of prodigious Advantage, in respect of their Manufactures, &c. and naval Power.

I have never had any Opportunity of attaining a satisfactory Account of the several Branches of this extensive Commerce, and Source of naval Power. But the Gold Dust brought from *Senegal* and *Goree*, must introduce a large Quantity of Bullion into *France*; as must the Gum, which is sufficient both to supply her own Manufactures, and a great Part, I fear, of ours; and, I believe, those of the *Dutch*:

Which muſt be paid for chiefly in Money. Indeed, I have heard this Article computed at 100,000*l. per Annum* to *France*. Elephants Teeth is likewiſe another valuable Branch of this Trade; which, when manufactured into numberleſs Utenſils and Toys, what of theſe are not uſed in *France*, being exported, bring back ſome Returns in Bullion or foreign Coin. Over and above theſe many and great Advantages, what, and how much greater, muſt ariſe to *France* from the Negro Trade, both in Reſpect of the Importation of Bullion, and the Demand of her Manufactures, and the Encreaſe of her People, and Improvement of her Agriculture, through ſuch an Encouragement of them? Moreover, the Advancement of the three laſt will be moſt alarming, if we duly conſider, that the Advancement of them muſt be proportionable to the Superiority of the *French* Trade, in Sugars, to that of the *Britiſh*.——For if *Great Britain* has only one-fifteenth Part of the Sugars exported, *France* muſt have fourteen Fifteenths; and, conſequently, the Number of Negroes, neceſſary to cultivate her Plantations, muſt be fourteen Times as many, as are required for the ſame Purpoſe in the *Britiſh:* And there cannot be leſs than fourteen Times as many Planters, to raiſe Sugars, Indigo, Ginger, Pimento, Cotton, and Coffee, in the *French* Sugar Settlements; to which we may add fourteen Times as may Ships, and Seamen, employed in that Trade: And the like Proportion of Manufactures, Artificers, and Huſbandmen, as are by *Great Britain.* What mighty Wealth muſt accrue to our faithleſs, perfidious, irreconcileable Enemy, from this moſt extenſive Traffic? What a Conſumption of her Manufactures, by the Goods, with which ſo many Negroes are bought, as are imported into *New Spain*, and her own Sugar Plantations, and Northern Colonies; and alſo as are required to cloath her own Negroes, and Planters? What a Conſumption of Manufactures, and of the Produce of Lands at Home, muſt the Cloathing and Feeding ſo many induſtrious Peo-

ple

ple and Seamen create? What a swift Progress must *France*, the universal Enemy of Mankind, make in internal and external Strength, under such numerous and mighty commercial Blessings? How soon will her dreadful Fleets overspread the Ocean for our utter Extirpation; and her destroying Armies subdue the other Powers of *Europe?*

In this most prosperous Condition, in this fair Way of accomplishing our Ruin, and her long projected Scheme of universal Monarchy, was *France* before the present War.—In the Reverse, sad, and desponding Condition, was poor unhappy, languishing *Britain*; exhausted of her small Profits upon her Commerce, vastly inferior to those of her treacherous and implacable Foe,—exhausted of most of her Specie in Subsidies to foreign Princes to promote *H—r—n* Interests; again exhausted of her Specie, and the stoutest of her People, to the Neglect of her Manufactures, Commerce, and Agriculture: wherein they were much wanted, and are now much missed; and for no other End, than for the first to be lavished, and the last to be slaughtered in *Germany*, for the Security of *H——r*, the original Cause of our Wars: *France* being encouraged by a ministerial Preference of the Electorate to this Nation, to break the Peace of *Utrecht*, invade and besiege our *American* Rights and Possessions; after having first, even in Time of profound Peace, like Thieves, clandestinely stolen and purloined such Valuables in that Region, as they would not have dared to touch with a Finger, if they had not been heartened to the Attempt, by their Assurance of that unnatural Preference of the Sons of *Britain:* Who, if they presumed, though in the humble Strains, to expostulate with the *French* Court against the Injustice of their Thefts, were instantly answered in the Style of Highwaymen. Deliver—or—we'll blow out your Brains; we will attack *H———r.—O spare us, spare us!* don't touch our Vitals, take all we have, only spare *H——r!* I say, in this prosperous Condition was *France*, before

fore the present War—In this sad, and desponding Condition was then *Great Britain:* When Providence, in Mercy to us, was pleased to raise up Mr. *Pitt* for our Deliverance.

He by the Wisdom of his Councils, by the uncorruptible Integrity of his Heart, by the invariable Firmness of his Resolution, and by the invincible Power of his mighty Genius, encountered and surmounted all our Difficulties; and freed us from all our Distresses and Perils, that had well nigh swallowed us up; and, as he and we all thought, set us upon a Rock of Security, out of the Reach both of our foreign and intestine Foes: And all this he did for us with the enormous Weight of continental Measures upon our Backs; while he himself *doubtless* sensible, as any Man, of their Fatality, was constrained publickly to espouse, what he must inwardly detest. He knew, that his Country must instantly perish under the crushing Load of continental Connections; that nothing could protract *her* Fall, but *that* of *France:* And, that the only Way to effect it, was to drive her intirely out of *America*; and, by gaining her Settlements, and engrossing her Commerce, enable this Nation, by the accruing Riches, to defray the heavy Charges of the *German* and *Gallic* Wars; and afterwards raise her naval Power and Grandeur to a higher State than ever: A Scheme so arduous and glorious, was far out of the Reach of the other Ministers Abilities. It was suited only to those of our Patriot, the great and wise Projector of it. Their shallow Penetrations could not comprehend an Object of that Magnitude. They could not conceive an Undertaking, pregnant with Uncertainty, could ever be attended with the Success that Experience hath taught them was possible and practicable. What therefore is reported, is probable to be true; that the Ministry, dreading the Power of Mr. *Pitt*'s Eloquence within Doors, and the Weight of his Popularity without, suffered him to make an Experiment which they thought impossible to succeed;

and

and which, if it should miscarry, would end in his Disgrace, and infallibly ruin his Credit and Interest with the People, under the Notion of his being a rash Projector. Mr. *Pitt* well knew, if he did not publickly support the continental System his Heart condemned, he should be driven from that Station, in which only he could execute his own great *American* Plan; the Success whereof could alone preserve his Country from unavoidable Perdition attending the *German* War, without the noble Acquisition of all *America*, consented to carry on continental Measures, odious to the whole Nation, even at a most exorbitant Expence; being absolutely certain, that his Opposition to them could neither have prevented the Measures, nor lessened the Expence. This, I hope, may be sufficient to vindicate the seeming Impropriety of this great and honest Statesman's Conduct, in this Particular; and to explain the finest Stroke of all his Eloquence; which being capable of a double Construction, hath been taken, by the People, in the Sense it was certainly designed to be taken by the Ministry; and hath, I am sorry to hear, lessened that high and just Esteem, and Affection for him, in the City, which his great Merits, and incomparable Services to the Nation, justly deserve from the Publick: And to which, when I have explained farther the Expression I allude to, I hope for your own, and your Country's Sakes, you will restore him in as ample a Degree as he lately enjoyed them.

His Expression was, if I have been rightly informed, "That *America* can only be conquered in *Germany*."—And where is the Absurdity, or Iniquity of this Maxim? Did Mr. *Pitt* ever avow, that spending *British* Blood and Treasure in *Germany*, was the only right Way of conquering *America*? Doth not the Expression imply plainly enough, that proper Measures would never be permitted by some Persons to be taken for the Conquest of *America*, unless the *German* War went Hand in Hand with it? The Expression is ambiguous, and may be construed in the

Manner

Manner it hath; that is, the only right Way of conquering *America:* But in this Ambiguity confifts the great Beauty of this Stroke of Eloquence, and the perfect Skill of the Speaker. At the Time that he conveys, or rather infinuates, to the Publick the Neceffity he is under of fupporting the continental Syftem, he could not prevent, in order to induce fome Perfons to agree to attempt the Conqueft of *America*; he effectually guards himfelf againft any malicious Conftruction of his Words by thofe, upon whofe Friendfhip he had perhaps little Reafon to depend.

Permit me then, my good and worthy old Friends and Mafters, to recommend to you that unviolable Love for Mr. *Pitt,* and that firm Confidence in his Integrity, which is not only due to him, for all the glorious Effects of his wife Adminiftration and unparallelled Virtues, but abfolutely neceffary for our inftant Prefervation in the prefent Danger; and for the future Security, Profperity, and Glory of this Country. For who is fo able, or willing, to refcue us out of the Hands of ignorant Pride and Ambition, when they expofe us to Ruin, as the M—n that has already refcued this Ifland out of the Hands of *France*; humbled that haughty Nation; reduced her tremendous Power to nothing; and laid her Glory in the Duft? Who is fo proper to be confided in, in Refpect either of Ability or Integrity, as the Man that hath protected our Merchants, and our Commerce; reftored our naval Power; and revived the fallen Honour of the *Britifh* Flag: Extended our Traffic to the moft diftant Regions of the Globe; put us in Poffeffion of a fourth Part of it; and made us once more Lords of the whole Ocean?

Can we ever flight fuch a Friend, without the Cenfure of Ingratitude; or by an unjuft Sufpicion debar ourfelves of the Affiftance of his Abilities and Fidelity, without the Imputation of Folly?

And fhall we then, my Lords and Sirs, when the Bill of Rights hath fo lately removed all Obftructions in the Passage to the Throne, and our Constitution opens an easy Access to both Houses of Parliament, stand by inactive, and behold silent all the mighty Blessings derived from Mr. *Pitt*'s honest and illustrious Administration, given back to a deceitful, insolent, and implacable Foe; only with the Dash of a Pen, guided by the Hand of Ignorance and Inability?—Shall we thus behold given back the Fruits of so much Toil, the Cost of Seas of Blood, and Mountains of Treasure?

But this brings me back from this long Digression, to consider all the Preliminaries, reported of the approaching Peace.

In doing which I shall endeavour to shew, that all the Preliminaries of Peace talked of, are in their Nature, and will be in their Consequence, destructive to the Commerce and national Independency of this Country; in-as-much as they must necessarily restore *France* to that internal and external Strength, wherein *Great Britain* found her at the Commencement of the present War: And if the over-hasty Temper of that Nation would have permitted a Forbearance of twenty or thirty Years longer, of the Exertion of that Strength, it would have got to such a Head, that nothing could have resisted it; and *Great Britain* must have been over-whelmed and lost for ever.

As the Riches and naval Power of *France*, arising from *America* and *Africa*, are the Bases, on which the Arguments to prove what I have above advanced, are built; it will not be improper to place before you, in one View, what has been hitherto dispersed in these Sheets, relative to the Importation of Bullion into *France*, by Means of their Sugar Plantations, the Fishery, and *Africa*; and also to place before you, in one View, the Increase of their naval Power, arising from those Branches of Commerce; and both compared with *Great Britain* in those Respects.

F *Sugar*

Sugar Plantations,

Great Britain.

Received for 5211 Hhds of Sugars from foreign Markets   81,422
—— for Indigo, Ginger, and other products, 16,284
———— 97,790
To balance   —   —   —   1,304,588

Newfoundland Fishery.

Received for Fish exported,   —   —   —   300,000
———— 300,000
To balance   —   —   —   1,050,000

Virginia and Maryland,

Received for 45,000 Hhds of Tobacco exported,   843,750
———— 843,750

Carolina.

Received for 000 Barrels of Rice exported,   80,000
———— 80,000
To balance in favour of *France*,   —   1,430,838

£. 2,752,294

North American Trade.

	Ships	Men.
In Tobacco	400	3600
In Rice	100	900
In the *Newfoundland* Fishery	300	8700
In the Rest of the Colonies,	300	2700

1100 — 15,900

Sugar Plantations.

Great Britain employs   —   26   240
——   ——   26 — 240
To balance in favour of *France*,   598 — 17,370

1724   33,510

Sugar Plantations.

France.

Received for 74,789 Hhds of Sugars from foreign Markets, } 1,168,578
—— for Indigo, Ginger, &c.   233,716
————— 1,402,294
By balance for 69,578 Hhds, &c. exported more than *Great Britain*, } 1,304,588

Newfoundland Fishery.
Received for Fish exported, - 1,350,000
————— 1,350,000
By balance in Exportation of more Fish than *Great Britain*, } 1,050,000

Virginia and Maryland.

Carolina.

£ 2,752,294

North American Trade.
	Ships	Men.
In the *Newfoundland* Fishery,	1344	30,096
In the rest of their Colonies,	6	54
		1350—30,150
France superior to *Britain*,	250	14,250

Sugar Plantations.
France employs -	374	3360		
			374	3,360
France superior to *Britain*,	348	3120		
			1,724	33,510

We see, in these Accounts of Bullion annually imported into *France*, and of the Increase of her naval Power, two *such* Ballances as are enough to strike every *Briton* with Amazement and Horror; and such, as one would imagine, must open the Eyes of the blindest Buzzard in the C—b—n—t; and soften the most obdurate Heart there, tho' harder than Adamant itself.

We see *Great Britain* before the War jostled by *French* Artifice and Industry, aided by *British* M—t—r—l Partiality for a foreign Territory, Negligence and Cowardice, out of two of the most valuable Branches of her Commerce, the Sugars, and the Fishery.—We see her naval Power daily declining, and that of *France* augmenting, by the almost intire Engrosment of these noble Branches of Trade; which raise and maintain such a Number of Seamen, the greatest Part of them being nurtured in that very Fishery; in which it is reported, we are going to give the *French* a right to Fish again, under such Restrictions, that we may be sure these renowned Treaty-Breakers will observe no longer, than they are too weak to break through them.

We see *France* with Regard to the Importation of Bullion, augmenting in Riches annually, by an Importation of it to the Amount of 2,752,294 *l.* and all arising only from their Sugar Plantations, and the Fishing in *our* Seas: of which immense Sum they received from the former 1,402,294*l.* and from the latter 1,350,000*l.* while poor unhappy *Britain*, the constant Prey of *France*, and the whole Continent of *Europe*; and the ever unnatural Sacrifice of her *own degenerate* Sons, imported from her reduced Sugar Plantations—from her own Fishery, and from all her Colonies in *North America*, no more than 1,321,456*l.* so that *France* before the War imported into *France*, from only their Plantations, and our Fishery 1,430,838*l.* more than

than *Great Britain* did from those two Sources of Wealth, and all her Northern Colonies besides.

And here I desire it may be observed, that tho' the *French* appear to be possessed of fourteen Times more of the *African* Trade, than we are; and, consequently, from it import fourteen times more Bullion, and grow fourteen Times more in naval Strength, than we do; Yet, for want of proper Information, I have brought nothing to the above Accounts, in Respect to either of these. But surely, if the Amount of Bullion imported into *France by*, and the Ships and Seamen employed *in* the *African* Trade, were to be added to the above Accounts, they would swell them greatly.

I shall now, my Lord and Sirs, consider the *famous* Preliminaries, said to be at this Time in Agitation; and endeavour to shew, in what Manner the above mentioned Ballance of Bullion, and Superiority in Ships and Seamen, will be affected by them. And then I believe, no honest *Briton* whatever will think himself obliged (if such Preliminaries are really in Agitation) in the least to our Illustrious Peace-Makers; or hold either their Abilities or Integrity in the least Veneration.

I freely own, that if upon the whole Trade of the World carried on by *Great Britain* and *France*, we had but as great a Ballance in our Favour, as appears to be only by suffering *France* to supply her home Consumption of Fish, the Ballance would in Point of Bullion imported, be rather in our Favour, if we could have an undoubted Security that that artful People, ever watchful over their own Interest, and ready to destroy their Neighbours, would not soon worm us out of it, through the Assistance of the Negligence, Ignorance, or perhaps Corruption of our future Ministers, in the same Manner they have hitherto done.

The Ballance in Favour of *Great Britain* upon the whole Trade of *America*, (*viz.*) the Plantations, Northern

Northern Colonies and the Fishery allowing for the home Consumption of Fish in *France* 600,000*l*. would be 369,162*l*. which if our whole Sale of Tobacco and Rice was to be paid for in Bullion, as it is not, since we purchase with it many Commodities, either useful in our Shipping or to supply our Luxury; in particular so much of our Tobacco, as we export to *France*, she pays for in Wines, &c. to the Value, as I have been informed, of 100,000*l*. Sterling. But as this must be, and ought to be deducted, it reduces the said 669,162*l*. to no more than 369,162*l*. And even this too depends upon our confining *France* to her home Consumption of *Mud Fish*; which we may be morally certain, we never shall. For as that Nation hath never scrupled to break all the Treaties, she bound herself by; whenever she thought herself strong enough to support the Violation of them, we cannot without the most foolish Credulity believe, she will Act with punctual Honour hereafter, or that our future Ministers will be more circumspect and careful than their Predecessors have been, to hold her to a strict Observance of the Restriction, of supplying her home Consumption only. Besides, *France*, by navigating cheaper, and the Situation of her Ports in *Europe* hath a double Advantage in serving *Portugal*, *Spain* and *Italy* cheaper, and throwing such Quantities into those Markets, occasionally as will render that Commodity a Dreg, and greatly lessen the Price of it. These Advantages will be an irresistible Temptation to *French* Faith, to fish for Baccaloa, and cure it on those Stages, and drying Rooms that are reported (since I began this Letter) to be allowed them on *Newfoundland*. Under this *Permission* they may load what Quantity of Baccaloa (which is the Sort of Fish only consumed by the *Portugueze*, *Spaniards*, and *Italians*,) in the Ships allowed them, together with Mud Fish for their own Consumption; which is what the *French* only consume. By the help of this, they may soon

turn

turn this small Balance in their own Favour, and will, in no long Time, again worm us out of the Fishery; for which we shall have no better Security, than the Faith of *France*, and the Wisdom, Fortitude, and Integrity of *British* Ministers: Who, if we may judge from past Experience, if the common Bully of *Europe* presents H―――r at them, as a Highwayman does a Pistol at a Traveller, will patiently suffer him to rob *Great Britain* of these her most valuable Rights and Possessions, or any other whatever.

And that *France* designs to recover this immense Source of Riches and Nursery of Seamen, in Consequence of this Preliminary, is (I think) indisputably manifest, from her *insisting* upon a *Permission* to erect *Stages*, and other Conveniencies, upon *Newfoundland*, for *drying* and *curing* her Fish. For if she intended nothing more than the *Supply* of her *Home Consumption*, she could have no *Occasion* for such *Stages* and drying Rooms; since she consumes only the *Mud* Fish: For which, *Stages* and drying Rooms are not *necessary*; whereas they are *absolutely so* for curing the Baccaloa, which is the *only* Consumption of *Portugal*, *Spain*, and *Italy*. Can then any Man be so completely stupid, as to imagine that *France*, if she did not *intend* and *hope* to supply those Markets again would desire a *Permission* to erect *Stages*, &c. to cure Baccaloa; and be at the Labour and Charge of thus preparing it, only to throw it away? And will our ingenious *Quid Nunc's* be so *easily* caught with a *French* Gudgeon?

It may not be improper here to forestal, what you will find in the Appendix; where you will see, that *France*, in *Charles* the First's Reign, paid an Acknowledgment of five *per Cent.* for the Permission of Fishing in those Seas; which is a Proof of the *Antiquity* of our *sole* Right in them; though she soon afterwards found Means to influence our Court so far, as to obtain a Remission of that Acknowledgment.

You

You will find also, that at the Peace of *Utrecht*, she had made so great a Progress in that Branch of Commerce, that she employed 400 Ships in it; which is 100 more than we employed before the present War. And since that Peace, she has made a most astonishing Progress therein, having encreased her Number of 400 Ships just mentioned to 1200 or 1500; which, at a Medium, is 1344 Ships *per Annum*. For if she sent to *North America* 1350, and employed only six Ships in her Colonies, the Residue 1344 could be used in no Part of that Region, but in the Fishery. And this proves the Verity of the *British Merchant*, who tells us in the Appendix, that the *French* are so extremely sensible of the *prodigious* Advantage of this *Fishery*, and so *very* intent upon pursuing it, that from their *first Attempt* to make themselves *considerable* at Sea, they had it *perpetually* in View.——And then if this be so, who will have the *Impudence* to deny, that they will have it *perpetually* in View, 'till by intirely divesting them of their whole *American* and *African* Trade, which last is an Appendage of the former, we shall have drawn out of the Teeth and Fangs of the voracious and insatiable Beast of Prey; which we ought to do, both for our own Preservation, and for that of the Rest of *Europe*: and this more especially we ought to do, since *France*, by *insisting* upon a *Permission* to erect *Stages* and other Conveniences on *Newfoundland* for curing *Baccaloa*, a Commodity suited only for the Markets of *Portugal*, *Spain*, and *Italy*, hath openly avowed her firm Resolution to drive *Great Britain* out of that most *enriching* Branch of her Commerce—and nursing Mother of her naval Power.

Moreover if we take into the Consideration the Restitution of *Goree*, the Possession whereof must, for the Reasons already enumerated, give *France* such a Superiority in the Profit of imported Bullion, that I doubt not in the least, it will reduce the above Balance of 269,162 *l.* supposed to be in our Favour, to an Equality, if not turn it against us. And in such a Case, will it not be an unexampled Instance of Weakness, Folly, Rashness, and Iniquity, to expose the Fate of this Country to the Hazard of an even Balance in Commerce with *France*.

And now, my Lord and Sirs, I have mentioned *Africa* again, permit me to offer you a few Remarks, particularly with respect to the Restitution of *Goree*.

Our Ministers, perhaps, may think they do a mighty Thing, if, when they restore *Goree*, they keep the Possession of *Senegal*; for that, by the Means of it, we shall at least equally divide the Profits of the rich and necessary Trade to *Africa* with our Enemy. If they should think so, they will find themselves under an egregious Mistake. But if they could be right in such a Conjecture, it would certainly be the Height of Madness, after so much Blood and Treasure spent to reduce the exorbitant and tremendous Power of *France*, as I said just now, to expose the Fate of this Country to the Hazard of an even Balance of any one Trade with *France*; or even to do so in respect of the universal Trade of the two Nations, as I shall endeavour to shew in its proper Place. But with respect to our Possession of *Senegal* without *Goree*, I cannot conceive how it can enter into the Heads of our *wise* Men, that either we shall reap any more Advantage from the *African* Trade, by the Possession of the one without the other, or that the *French* Trade will be in the least diminished by this Concession; which, without *Goree*, will be rather a Prejudice than a Benefit to *Great Britain*.

The Necessity of either Nations embarking in a Commerce with *Africa*, principally ariseth from the Impossibility of cultivating their Settlements in *America*, especially the Sugar Islands, without Negroes; though the Gums, Elephants Teeth, and Gold Dust might

might otherwife render it a very beneficial one. If then one Nation's Demand for Negroes is greater than the others, that Nation whofe Demand exceeds the others, will employ moft Ships and Seamen, and export moft Manufactures; and will thereby raife more Seamen and employ more Manufacturers, and proportionably encourage its Agriculture. Now *France* (as I have already faid) vending fourteen Times as much Sugar, Indigo, &c. as *Great Britain*, is, in all thefe Advantages attending this Trade, fourteen Times more confiderable than her; who, by the Poffeffion of *Senegal*, can purchafe no more Negroes than the Growth of her Settlements in *America* requires: And as fhe can have a fufficient Supply of them without *Senegal*, by the Conveniency of her own Forts and Settlements upon the Coaft of *Africa*, which afford fafe Harbours for her Ships and Store-houfes for her Goods, fhe does not want *Senegal* to carry on her Negroe Trade; the *African* Forts and Settlements not being Markets for Negroes, who, as I apprehend, are bought upon the Coafts in coafting Voyages.

Next let us inquire of what Ufe *Senegal* without *Goree* is likely to be to *Great Britain*, with refpect to the Traffic in Gums, Elephants Teeth, and Gold Duft; or in the Diminution of the *French* Negroe Trade. The Ships employed by the *Britifh* Merchants, being only in Proportion to their Share in the *American* Intereft, they will fend but one in fifteen; and the Manufactures to purchafe the Commodities above fpecified, being conveyed in the fame Ships that convey thofe that purchafe Negroes, there can be fent but one fifteenth Part of our Manufactures to barter away for Gums, Elephants Teeth, and Gold Duft: So then the *French* having fourteen Fifteenths of the Negro Trade, will fend fourteen Times the Number of Ships that *Great Britain* can, and confe-
quently

quently fourteen Times the Quantity of Manufactures to barter away for the fame Commodities; and muſt therefore load for *France* fourteen times the Quantity of thoſe valuable Effects, wherewith ſhe muſt gain fourteen times as much as *Great Britain*.

France alſo hath another great Advantage over us herein:—ſhe Manufactures her Goods ſo much cheaper than *Great Britain*, that ſhe is able to out bid her 25 *per Cent*. And if theſe are Facts, how will it be poſſible for this Nation, to ſhare equally theſe prodigious Advantages, with our Rival and Enemy?

Goree of itſelf is, doubtleſs, ſufficient for the Negroe Trade, and the foregoing Reaſons ſecure them in a Manner, in the intire Poſſeſſion of the other Branches of the *African* Commerce. Otherwiſe, we may be ſure *French* Modeſty would not have hindered the *French* Court demanding *Senegal* as well as *Goree*. And what Reaſon have we to believe the good Nature of our M——y would have denied any Demand, that it ſhould have made? *Senegal* therefore without *Goree* will be an uſeleſs Expence to this Nation. And as *Goree* is ſufficient to anſwer all the Purpoſes of that Trade to *France*, it is no wonder ſhe ſhould readily make us a Conceſſion uſeleſs and expenſive to its Poſſeſſor. Thus we ſee that *Senegal* without *Goree* cannot give us half the Trade of *Africa*, if our M———s did really intend their Country ſo much good. So here we ſee another *French* Gudgeon thrown out to catch the *Britiſh* Miniſtry.

Nothing ſurely can equal their Generoſity and Charity, if there is Truth in the Preliminaries publiſhed. A Right of fiſhing in our *American* Seas for their home Conſumption, and an Opportunity of enriching themſelves and Augmenting their Maritime Power, by permitting them to erect Stages, *&c.* for curing Baccaloa for the Uſe of *Portugal*, *Spain*, and *Italy*, which will enable them to drive us out of the Fiſhery,

is much too mean a Present for the *French* King.—
So trifling an Offering is much beneath the Dignity
of *Louis Le Grand*. To render the M———l Present acceptable to him, it can be accompanied with
nothing less, than those valuable Sugar Islands, whose
whole Products cannot be worth less than upwards of
1,000,000*l*. Sterling *per Annum* in *France*, together with
Goree. Which, if we reckon the value of the Negroes,
with all the other Branches of that Commerce, may
reasonably be estimated at 1,000,000*l*. more; in all
2,000 000*l*. Sterling *per Annum*. All rich Jewels torn
from the Crown of *France*, by that hard-hearted,
cruel, vindictive, inexorable *Robber* Mr Pitt, who
bearing an Implacable Hatred to *Lewis* the XVth. for
no better Reasons, than that *Lewis* the XVth. bore the
same implacable Hatred to Mr. Pitt's Country, and
had first stolen and seized some of the Jewels out of
his own Royal Master's Crown, and was bent upon
taking away all the rest.

But to return to the Value of our Present, to his
Most Christian Majesty. This 2,000,000*l*. being added to the Value of their home Consumption of Fish,
caught in our Seas, will make the Donation worth about 2,600,000 *l. per Annum*, besides an immediate
and large Nursery for *French* Seamen, and an Opportunity of recovering what we retain of it by Treaty:
which, we may be sure they will break as soon as they
can; because we know they have broke every Treaty
they have made with us. Now can there be a more
noble Instance either of Generosity or Charity, than
to give up no less than 2,600,000*l. per Annum* for no
Consideration; and voluntarily, and without Power
in him to whom we give it, to take it from us. Therefore as we are under no Compulsion, it can proceed
from nothing but pure and perfect Generosity. O generous Souls! All the World must own and admire
it, tho' I believe, not any State whatever would follow

so

so good an Example.—Nor is our Charity less pure and perfect;—for it is an Exuberance, even of Christian Charity.—*That* only commands Forgiveness of our Enemy upon Repentance and Reparation, and to do good for Evil.—But it doth not bid us give him all we are worth, nor to put a Weapon into the Hands of him, we know to be an implacable Enemy, that would cut our Throats with it, as soon as he got Possession of it. Yet so excessively Charitable are we, that tho' we are certain, *France* will turn our Charity to our Destruction, we most charitably put ourselves into the Power of our implacable and most uncharitable Enemy.

How far doth the Charity of some *Britons* exceed that of the Merciful *Samaritan*, so highly applauded by the highest Authority! The *Samaritan*'s Charity extended no further, than to a single *Jew*; between whose Nation and his own, though a perpetual Grudge subsisted, it does not appear, that *Samaria* had been unjustly invaded, pillaged, and most inhumanly treated by the *Jews*, in Breach of solemn Treaties. But if the Preliminaries are true, the far more than Christian Charity of our most merciful *Samaritans*, will be extended to Sixteen Millions of Strangers, our antient, inveterate, and irreconcileable Enemies, who have been justly punished for their Robberies and barbarous Murders committed upon us in Breach of solemn Treaties. The antient *Samaritan*, after he had poured Oil and Wine into the Wounds, of the unfortunate *Jew*, and lodged him in an Inn, gave the Host only Two-pence, promising to pay all other Charges for the Relief of the wounded Stranger; which it is likely might amount to Two pence or a Groat more. But our *Samaritans*, infinitely more merciful and generous, can give the wounded *French*, who got their Wounds in endeavouring to wound us, no less than about 2,600,000*l*.

per

per Annum, sterling, immediately, together with the Means of acquiring the whole Trade of the World and becoming the sole maritime Power.

What can induce us to this impolitic Work of charitable Supererogation, I own I am at no small Loss to guess; unless it be, that our *wise* Men think that because we are to treat with the Most *Christian King*, therefore we are to rival him in Christian Appellation, and are resolved to merit *that* of the most Christian Dupes.

We have in *England* a Phrase, usually applied to Acts of extreme Folly, when it is improper to laugh out at them, that very properly expresseth the inward Contempt of a By-stander—we are apt to say, such a one "laughs in his Sleeve." And if there is Truth in the published Preliminaries, surely *Nivernois* cannot forbear laughing in *his* Sleeve at the amazing Conduct of our *renowned* Politicians.—Methinks I see the *sensible* and *honest* FRENCHMAN, in his *private* Apartment, TRIUMPHING over their Understandings.—Methinks I see him, with all the Vivacity natural to his Climate, in the highest Transports of Joy, clapping his Hands, and capering about his Room—and, methinks, I hear him bursting out in such Exclamations as these upon his Success: "O happy *France*, art thou then so unexpectedly delivered out of thy Conqueror's Hands! O my fortunate Country, hath thy injured Enemy, flushed with repeated Victories over *thee*, reduced to the last Extremity, by the Courage of the *British* Arms by Sea and Land, spared *thee* after so many Conquests!—And do I see her trembling at thy haughty Threats, tamely submissive to thy Dictates, at the Instant—at the very Instant thou liest gasping and expiring under her Feet! O *France*, O my dear Country, thou art now safe, and shalt soon be great again! O my Prince, my royal Master, thou shalt soon arrive at the high

Pinnacle of Glory, whither thy ambitious Predecessors in *vain* aspired! The two Branches of the House of *Bourbon* are now united, we have now by Peace reduced *Old England*, *that heretofore* unsurmountable Obstacle to our mighty Object of universal Sway.—If she, by *our pretending* to relinquish the *Newfoundlan* Fishery, all but our Home Consumption, *should* for a Time enjoy an equal Share of the Profits of the Trade to *America*, or even a small Balance in her Favour, *that* Advantage will be of a short Duration. Baccaloa cured on the Stages and Rooms erected on *Newfoundland*, will soon run away with her Profits, and restore to *France* her former Balance of Trade 1,430,838 *l.* and that great Nursery of Seamen. O brave! O brave!—30,000 Seamen to be released to man a new formidable Fleet! O brave again! Our Marine will soon be strong enough to face the *British*.——But hold—let me think—ah—now I have it—we must be *good* Friends and Neighbours with *Great Britain*; at least for some Time: For having bound her fast Hand and Foot by this Peace, in consequence whereof we shall, with the *united* Fleets of the *united* Branches of the House of *Bourbon*, soon dethrone the King of *Portugal*: And, by giving that Kingdom to the King of *Spain*, we shall get Possession of not only the whole Trade of *Old* and *New Spain*, but the *Brazils* too will be ours. Thus we shall import all the Bullion of those prodigious wide extended Regions into *France*.—Why—besides the vast Wealth accruing to *Great Britain* from their Commerce with *Spain*, we shall, by such a Blow given to the King of *Portugal*, at once strip that Land of Heretics of at least 1,000,000*l.* Sterling *per Annum*, which will all come to *France*. By this too, while her naval Strength daily declines with her Manufactures, in Proportion as ours increase, the Poor of *Great Britain* must starve or fly to *France* for Bread.—Well—Bread they shall have

have—and Bread made of Corn the Growth of their *native* Soil.—But it shall be raised by *Frenchmen*; large Colonies of whom we must transplant thither. So then they *shall* eat the *Bread* of *British* Corn:—But they shall earn it *dear*—very dear—they shall *hew* Wood and *draw* Water for us, and sweep our Streets and cleanse our Kennels. And these servile Offices for us Slaves, shall these *boasting* free-born *Britons* perform, hampered in *French* wooden Shoes—and loaded with ponderous Chains—and galled with corroding Fetters.—And by that Time we have reduced *Holland* to our Obedience, and added all her Spice Settlements in the *East Indies* to *Pondicherry*, the kind Concession of good natured unforeseeing *Britain*, and have engrossed all the Commerce of the *Dutch*, by which we shall be Masters of all the Wealth of the Universe, and of numerous and well-manned Squadrons, that will overspread the whole Ocean; *Great Britain* exhausted of her Riches, and drained of her Inhabitants, will, with the poor Remnant of her once dreadful and all-victorious Fleets, make but a *feeble* Resistance, to the superb naval Force of *France*.

"It will then be Time to invade her, and take away her Name and her Place, and lead away Captive, with their Wives and little Ones, those who do not come to us of their own Accord.—The three richest commercial States, *Portugal, Holland,* and *Great Britain,* (the two last the greatest naval Powers) being thus totally subdued, the other States of *Europe* will soon be brought to submit and bear the Yoke. *Sardinia*, however wise and valiant her Sovereign may be, assaulted by the House of *Bourbon*, cannot long bear up against a Force so greatly superior.—In *Italy*, the King of *Spain* has a strong Hold through the Kingdom of *Naples*, which will help forwards the Reduction of *Italy*; and the House of *Austria*, whom we have politically joined, in order to impoverish it by

exhausting

exhausting its Wealth in a rash War, can withstand the *French* and *Spanish* Powers but a little While. Nor will the military Abilities of the *Prussian* Hero, avail him against the same united Forces.

"Thus, by the Subversion of these mighty States, my Master's Power becoming invincible; the hardy *Swede*, without a Fleet, and not over-flushed with Wealth, will fall an easy Victim to the glorious Ambition of *my* Sovereign: And little *Denmark*, will scarce suffice him for a Breakfast.——But—I did not think of the paltry Principalities of *Germany*;—indeed they are scarce worth my Notice—but, however, these Baubles may do well enough to distribute amongst my Master's Ladies—They may serve Madam *Pompadour* and the rest, in the Hours of Dalliance, for Sugar Plumbs and Carraways——*Pompadour*, may be made Dutchess of *Munster*—another, Marchioness of *Mentz*—another, Countess of *Cologne*—another, Viscountess *Triers*—and---another---may be made—— Baroness of *Hanover*: But enough of this. The infidel *Turk*, in no Condition to oppose our overgrown Strength, will soon acknowledge him for their Lord. And though the Intrepidity of the stout *Russians* may hold us a While in play, they too, like the Rest of the Powers of *Europe*, must fall under the Feet of *Louis*, and submit their Necks to the Iron Yoke of *France*.

"Thus three Quarters of the World will soon be under the Dominion of *Louis le Grand*. *Asia* the Fourth, over-spread with a luxurious effeminate Race, undisciplined, and not much inured to War, will fall an easy Conquest to us *valiant FRENCHMEN*.—— O raré *France!* O rare *France!*—What, *Louis le Grand*, sole Monarch of the whole World. O rare *France!*——Well—I do not despair of this, if I can with a Dash of a *British* Pen—put into my Hands by the S———nts of the *British* C———n, counter-sign these Preliminaries. Then will be laid a sure Foundation of the univerfal Monarchy of *France*; and when the noble Structure is raifed, then fhall all the enflaved Inhabiters of the Earth, trembling, revere *le Grand* Monarch, and pay implicit Obedience to his dreadful Nod. O rare *France!*—And O thou my Pen, thou dear *Britifh* Deftroyer of *Britain*'s Commerce, of *Britain*'s naval Power, of *Britain*'s Fame and Independency upon *France*—thou, bleffed Reftorer of the ruined Fortunes and loft Honour of my Royal Mafter, and my beloved Country, fhalt inclofed in a Cafe of pureft Gold, curioufly chafed and fet with the brighteft oriental Stones, defcend, with my Titles and Eftate, to my lateft Pofterity, as a Jewel of ineftimable Price.—And thou precious Inftrument of my immortal Glory, tell me if thou can'ft, of *what* Materials the Heads of fome Folks are formed? This, indeed I know full well, that—there is not---*one* Conjurer amongft them all. I am almoft tempted to think, either that they fprung from Eggs, hatched under that Kind of Bird, on whofe Pinion thou didft grow; or that their Dams, allured by fome Male of the fame Species, conceived them as *Leda* conceived, when fhe refigned her Charms to the Swan.

" Well—next to the Love of God, the Love of our Country is, furely, the moft *noble* and glorious of all the moral Duties and human Paffions.—The meer Profpect of performing the leaft Service to our *native* Country, exhilerates the Heart of the honeft Man, and yields him an Extacy of Joy that infinitely exceeds all the higheft Pleafures of Luxury, Avarice, Vanity, or falfe Ambition——But to reach out to her *(*like *Pitt,* in whofe Head and Heart refide all the Abilities and Virtues of the *Grecian, Roman,* and *Britifh* Patriots) a friendly and faving Hand, when fhe ftands trembling and pale upon the Verge of Annihilation, is a Joy that tranfports and ravifhes my Heart to a Degree beyond the Reach of
Expreffion,

Expreſſion, and *ſurely* can be *no faint* Anticipation of that Portion of eternal Bliſs aſſigned for the Reward of uncorrupt Patriots; who, doubtleſs, in thoſe Regions of unfading Glory, ſhall ſit for ever high enthroned, next to the holy Apoſtles and the glorious Army of Martyrs.—O that my Dagger could give a mortal Wound to *Britannia*'s Heart! then would my glad Soul willingly ſoar to thoſe happy Seats, whereto no *Enemy* to his Country can ever arrive.—If then the faithful ſerving ones Country, affords the moſt exquiſite Delight, and is attended with ſo much Luſtre of Character upon Earth, and is diſtinguiſhed with infinite Felicity and Glory in Heaven—what a Reverſe of Anxiety, what Infamy of Character, and Portion of the ſharpeſt Pangs of Damnation, muſt await the Wretch that ſhall betray his Country, or ſervilely flatter the peccant Humours of his Prince! —rather than ſtain his Name *with* ſuch *foul* Deeds, let *Nivernois* periſh by ten Thouſand Tortures.—By St. *Peter*, and all the Apoſtles—by every Saint above —by my Crucifix—by all the holy Relicts in the *Vatican*, and by his Holineſs himſelf, Heaven's awful and infallible Vicegerent on Earth—I ſwear—if I thought my Tongue ever capable of aſſenting to, or my Hand of ſigning one ſingle Article the leaſt prejudicial, or diſhonourable to *France*—the *one*, I would pluck out by the Roots—and the *other*, behold with the Firmneſs of *Mutius Scævola*—wither in a Flame."

Here, my Lord and Sirs, we will leave honeſt *Nivernois* to his Soliloquy—with which I ſhould not have troubled you, if it was not my real Opinion that they ſuggeſt too many melancholy Truths not impoſſible to come to paſs.

But to return, you will pleaſe to obſerve, that the preceding Computations, ſo far as they reſpect the Importation of Bullion into *Great Britain* and *France*, are built upon a Suppoſition that all the Products ariſing from the ſeveral Branches heretofore-mentioned,

tioned are fold by both Nations for foreign Coin or Bullion. Which is not really the Cafe of either; tho' *France* muft, I think, have greatly the Advantage in this Refpect, becaufe fhe has, within herfelf, fo many more of thofe Commodities ufeful and neceffary for Manufactures, and to fupply Luxury, without importing them from foreign Countries than *Great Britain*, who, therefore, is obliged to import the former; and her Folly drives her to do the fame with Refpect to the latter. Even upon this Suppofition *France* had before the War a monftrous Ballance in her Favour, and upon the fame Suppofition upon the Peace, of our Returns being made in Bullion for all our Rice and Tobacco exported, only deducting 100,000*l*. for the Quantity fent to *France*, by giving them right to fifh for their home Confumption we fee no more than a Ballance of 269,162*l*. in our Favour, upon a vain Prefumption, that we fhall remain in Poffeffion of the *Portugal*, *Spanifh* and *Italian* Markets for Baccaloa; which it is very evident (as hath been before obferved) the *French* do not mean we fhall do, by their defiring Stages ufeful for that Sort of Fifh, which is only vendable in thofe Markets; fo that when they once regain that Branch of the Fifhery, they will be upon the fame footing, with Refpect to the Ballance of the *American* Trade, they were before the War: but if not, their Superiority of the *African* would ftill turn the Ballance in their favour. And can any Man think it expedient, to make a Peace with *France*, with a Ballance of Trade in her Favour in any Degree or Shape whatever?

But if we confider the univerfal Trade, carried on by both Nations before the War, we fhall, I fear, have too much Reafon to believe the Ballance of Trade, to have been greatly in Favour of *France*. And if fo, we ought never to reft, till we have driven her quite out of *America*; for by that only, we can effectually fecure the Ballance of Trade in our Favour, and keep down her naval Power. And if we neglect

to

to do so, now Providence hath put it in our Power, we must be the first Victim, to the boundless Ambition of the common Enemy of Mankind:—And the Corner-stone of her universal Monarchy.

To form such a State of the Balance of Trade between the two Nations, as will come nearest to the Truth, is not to be done by any one Man, especially by me, who am so far removed from the trading Parts of this Island. I can only offer my Reasons, why I think the Ballance of Trade in general was before the War, in Favour of *France*. Whether it was so or not, ought to be, with Regard to making Peace or carrying on the War against her, the first Consideration with our Administration: Since upon their Resolves, the Fate of this Country depends. And therefore I earnestly wish, that the most considerable Merchants of the City of *London*, would agree to meet and draw out a State of the Trade of both *Great Britain* and *France*, and Strike a Ballance, as correct as the Nature of the thing will permit, for the Information of the Administration and the Parliament; that this Poor Island may not be totally lost for Want of it. That this good and necessary Work may be as correct as possible, I hope all the Merchants of the Out Ports, will lend a helping Hand to it, either by their Attendance in *London* or by Correspondence. In the mean while I shall take the Liberty, agreeable to what I lately proposed, to offer such Reasons as occur to me upon this Head.

First then, tho' I have supposed hitherto, that our Return for all our Products of *America* are made in Bullion, it is not really so. But my Intention in stating the foregoing Accounts upon this Supposition was to heighten, as much as possible the Profits of this Country's Trade; that after all that can be said, to set it in the most favourable Light to *Britain*, she will still appear to be upon such a Footing with *France*, in the Point of Importation of Bullion and the *American*

rican Commerce, that the making a Peace upon the Preliminaries published, must bring the Trade and naval Power of this Nation and its Independency upon *France*, into so precarious and dangerous a Situation, as cannot be justified by any one Principle of Policy or Honesty.

The foregoing State of Bullion imported into the two Nations, is now to be laid aside in forming a Judgment, whether upon the general Trade carried on by both, the Ballance lies on the side of *Great-Britain* or *France*. All besides, that hath been said upon the Products of the Sugar Plantations, *North America* and of the *Newfoundland* Fishery, and *Africa*, are to be remembered upon this Head, being of equal Force in the present and last Argument; with this Difference only, that whereas we valued the Sugars and Tobacco at what they sold for in foreign Markets, upon the Exportation, we shall now only estimate them at prime Cost in the Mother Countries.

I pass over the home Consumption of both Nations as only serving chiefly to employ their own People.

First, we will consider the Products of *America* and *Africa*.

Great Britain imported before the War, from her northern Colonies, for Exportation to foreign Markets,

	£.
Tobacco, Hogsheads 45,000, at 15*l.* per Hhd in *Great Britain*, about	675,000
Rice 50,000 Barrels, Ditto, about	80,000
Fishery, Train Oil, and Whale-bone	300,000
From her Sugar Plantations, Hogsheads Value Ditto 12*l.* 10*s.*	65,137
Other Products from Ditto one-fifth Value of Sugars, about	13,025
	1,133,162

France

France.   £.
From the Fishery Train Oil and Whale-bone   1,350,000
         Sugar Plantations.
74,787 Hhds, at 12*l.* 10*s. per* Hhd at Home   934,863
Other Products about ———   ———   186,972
                                                      ————————
                                                       2,471,835
                                                       1,133,162
                                                      ————————
         Ballance in Favour of *France*   1,338,673

From *America* then what a great Advantage *France* had over *Great Britain*, in rich Commodities for Exportation to foreign Markets in *Europe*, appears from this short State of the Quantities and Value of imported Products, *viz.* no less than a Superiority of 1,338,673 *l. per Annum* Sterling, prime Cost: and this, exclusive of the Superiority, she had over Aby the Importation of Gums and Elephants Teeth from *Africa*. In this Place I take no Notice of her Importation of Gold Dust imported from thence; nor of the Silver imported by her from *New Spain*, in Return for Negroes, *&c.* We shall make a Remark on these hereafter.——But with respect to Gums and Elephants Teeth, let it be remembered, fourteen Times as much more as *Great Britain* can import, was imported by *France* before the War. All these Products brought from *America* and *Africa* ought to be esteemed as the Products of *France*, in as much as they are from her own Colonies and Settlements, and are raised by *French* Hands, or bought with *French* Manufactures; and all carried in *French* Bottoms, navigated by *French* Seamen.

Now Commerce in general may be thus defined: — It is an Exportation of the Staples, and Manufactures, and Products of one Country to other Countries, to be there bartered away either for their Money,—or for such of their Manufactures, Materials, and Products

ducts as either are necessary in working up her own Manufactures, or are for her Subsistance or Conveniency.

This then being granted, it will necessarily follow, that the Greatness or Smalness of any Nation's Trade will depend upon the Number of her Staples, Manufactures, Materials, and Products within itself; and that the Nation, that hath most of these within herself, will enjoy the greatest Share of Trade; not only by the employing a greater Number of Hands, but by an Importation of more Bullion: For as she will sell the Surplus of her own Consumption of her Staples, Manufactures, Materials, and Products to Foreigners that want them, she will have more Returns in Bullion than other Nations, that not having the same Advantages, or at least in the same Degree within themselves, are obliged to import them from their Neighbours, whilst she, also wanting fewer, Things from her Neighbours, has less Occasion to send out her Money.

Therefore when two Nations rival each other in Trade, though it may be very difficult to discover the exact Sum or Amount of the Ballance in Favour of the Nation where it lies, it will be very easy to find on which Side the Ballance really is; for that, that has within itself most of the Advantages just now enumerated, will have greater Exportations of Goods and Products, and greater Importations of Bullion, and fewer Occasions of exporting it again.

The great Rivalship of Trade before the War, lay between *Great Britain* and *France*. That Rivalship the Successes of the War has determined; if it is not revived by a Peace with our Rival; especially by one agreeable to the strange Preliminaries published, which, to the national Astonishment, have never been contradicted. But the Contest will be of no long Duration; for our Rival will soon engross the whole Trade, that was lately carried on between the two Nations; if ever the ill-judged Charity of our most charitable and merciful *Samaritans*, shall restore our
rival

rival Enemy to that greatly superior and formidable Strength, from which that most uncharitable and unmerciful Man, Mr. *Pitt*, reduced her, upon the strange and unfashionable Notion of prefering the Interest of his King and Country, either to that of *France* or of himself.

But whether the Ballance lay in Favour of *Great Britain* or *France* before the War, will appear by an Enquiry into the Manufactures, Materials, and Products of each Nation within itself.

We have already seen, that *France*, by almost the sole Possession of the Sugar and Fish Commerce, has at least 2,471,835 l. *Great Britain*, by a few Sugars and Fish, and all the Tobacco Commerce, only 1,133,162l. So that *France* hath in Products for supplying the foreign Markets a greater Stock than *Great Britain*, to the Value of 1,338,673l. and as to Gums and Elephants Teeth, she has fourteen Times more than *Great Britain*. *France* and *Great Britain* hath both Silk Manufactures, but *France* produces all her raw Silk for that Manufacture. We buy, for the same Use, all ours of *Piedmont*, for which we pay 100,000l. *per Annum* ; and of *Turkey*, which lets us have it for our Manufactures. *France* produces Wine, Brandy, and Olives; great Quantities of which she exports. We have none. If we have Corn sufficient for ourselves and Exportation, she, by converting many of her Vineyards to Arable, has the same; and though the Growth is not so good as ours, by underselling us at *Lisbon* and other Markets, 25 or 30 *per Cent*. she has a Share of that Exportation, as I have been well informed by the late Mr. *Burrel*, a very considerable Merchant, and an honest Gentleman, who had an old established House at *Lisbon*. *France* has a considerable Manufacture in Hats. We have the same, we had it from her.——Coals we have: She has none, but can have them from us cheap enough to manufacture her Iron so reasonable, that, by the

greater

greater Cheapness of her Labour, she is able to export her manufactured Iron at a much lower Price than we can. France has an Exportation for printed, Table, and wearing Linens.——We have in *Scotland* and *Ireland* the same; but yet it is, I believe, scarce sufficient for our own Consumption; and, I fear, we shall hardly be able to get the foreign Market out of the Hands of *France*, *Holland*, and *Hamburgh*. France may want naval Stores from her Neighbours, as well as Great Britain, and, I fear, she will soon have a larger Want of them. These are purchased with Money by both. The Woollen Trade she has almost got from us: She almost intirely supplies *Turkey* with Woollen Goods; and if we did not take off their Wines, and Oil, and Fruits, she would worm us out of the *Portugal* and *Spanish* Consumption of our Woollen Goods. I fear she interferes not a little with us in the latter, and will probably much more, now the Houses of *Bourbon* are united. France certainly uses much of our Wool in her Manufactures: But for it, she gives us nothing but her Wines, her Brandies, many of her Silks, and, I am sorry to say, some of her Woollen Goods; by which she gets more in foreign Markets, than the Cost of the Wool: For when I had the Honour to sit in Parliament, I have seen Courtiers in that Assembly, in French Cloth trimm'd with French Lace: even the Man, that was afterwards called by that unconstitutional Name of first Minister. So great an Aversion did some seem to have to their *native* Country, that they could not bear to encourage her Manufactures.

It would be endless to mention every Particular of the internal Advantage, *France* has over us. I hope to see all of them set forth, by our most worthy and respectable Body of Merchants, in the great and necessary Work I have, in these Sheets, taken the Liberty to recommend to them; and which I do now again, for the Sake of themselves, their Country, and

latest

latest Posterity. For if the Preliminaries published are true, and a Peace is to be concluded agreeable to them, this Nation, I do verily believe, much within the Space of a Century, will neither be a trading Nation, nor an independant one upon *France*.

Let it suffice then for the present, that *France* having almost every Thing within herself, wants little or nothing from other Countries, and therefore taking little or nothing from them, must have her Returns mostly in Bullion; and more especially as her Exports are greatly to *Spain*, and the *Spanish West Indies*, and *Italy*. Besides that she imports an immense Quantity of Bullion in Gold Dust, for Returns for Goods sent to *Africa*, and in Silver for Negroes sold to *New Spain*, which Negroes are purchased with *French* Manufactures. Whereas *Great Britain* wanting many Things for necessary Uses, particularly in her Shipping and Manufactures, even Gums, which she purchases of *France*, as I have been told, and making fewer Manufactures and consequently vending fewer;--besides paying vast Interest for 30,000,000*l*. of Debt to Foreigners, and immense Sums to *France* for Wines and other Things, together with what is spent there by *British* Fools that go thither to collect and import *French* Follies, our Imports of Bullion must be very small in Comparison with those of *France*. So that, if we do not intirely destroy her Trade in *America* and *Africa*, before we allow her Peace, she must become much the greater commercial and naval Power, which must end in the utter Ruin of *Great Britain*.

My Lord and Sirs, I have detained you a long while, from the Consideration of the important Part of the published Preliminaries that respects the Restitution of *Guadaloupe* singly, or that of all the conquered Sugar Islands.

It was first reported, that we were to restore *Guadaloupe*, together with *Goree*. But soon afterwards by the Preliminaries divulged in the *Evening Post* before mentioned, we are informed, not only *Guadaloupe*, but *Marigalante*, *St Lucia*, and *Martinico* were to be reftored too; which laft is of the utmoft Confequence to *France*, as it has a moft noble Harbour for Privateers to lye ready, to pop out and take all our trading Ships in Time of War, and which muft be of equal Confequence to *Great Britain*, as the Poffeffion of it is both a Protection to her *Weft India* Trade, and gives her the like Opportunity of diftreffing that of the *French*; if the driving *France* quite out of *America*, fhould be fo abfolutely incompatible with the exuberant Charity of our moft charitable and merciful *Samoritans*, that they are determined not to do, what is abfolutely neceffary, for the Security of the Trade and *national* Exiftence of their *native* Country.

If we recollect what has been faid in the preceding Pages, relating to the Confumption of Sugars, Indigo, &c. in the foreign Markets, and the Reafons that have thrown that profitable Trade, into the Hands of *France*, we cannot but clearly fee, that (as I early obferved) the Difference of reftoring *Guadaloupe* only, or all the conquered Iflands, is no more than this: If we give up that, it will be a few Years only, before *France* will be able to raife the Quantity of the 80,000 Hogfheads of Sugar and other Products taken off by the foreign Markets. If we give them up all the reft, that are mentioned, they will immediately engrofs that whole Commerce, to the very great *Damage* of this Nation. So that the Reftitution of *Guadaloupe* alone, will only protract, not prevent the Ruin of the Sugar Commerce with Regard to this Country.

To illuftrate this Truth, it will be proper to obferve, that a great Number of Iflands are not fo neceffary for this Purpofe, as the Extent and Fertility of one, efpecially if the different Parts of one Ifland will produce the feveral different Sorts of Sugar required in the Markets. If it will not, then as many other

other Islands would be requisite as would produce the several Sorts. Otherwise the fewer Islands any Nation hath, the better; if the hindering others from taking Possession of the vacant, in order to keep them out of that Trade, was not an unanswerable Argument for keeping all. Because, the national Charge of fortifying and garrisoning many must be immensely greater, than of one or two. Especially, as the doing this to each must be full sufficient for the Defence of each; and whatever Charge would attend any single Island, the same would attend every one, unless where the Natural Strength of any should contribute in some Degree to lessen it. Moreover, a single Island would be impregnable, from the internal Strength it would acquire, from the several Inhabitants dispersed over many, being collected into one aggregated Body.

If this be true, and supposing *Guadeloupe* to have Soils adapted to the several Species of Sugars required by the Markets, *Guadeloupe* is, itself, sufficient to raise enough, both to answer the foreign Demand and the home Consumption of *France*. It is said, that not one tenth Part of it is cultivated, and what is, produces annually 40,000 *French* Hogsheads of Sugar; which may be about 24,000 of *English*: So that, if this Island was thoroughly improved, it would produce 248,000 *English* Hogsheads: which is 160,000 more than the foreign Demand, besides Indigo &c. insomuch that *France* would have yearly, after supplying the foreign Demand and her home Consumption, a great Surplus upon her Hands. Moreover, the *French* Planters of the other Islands, were these to be left in our Possession, flocking to *Guadaloupe*, would in a few Years improve it enough, to answer all the Purposes of the Mother Country; and render it too strong to be retaken by us, in a future War. But if the Soil of this Island should be only adapted to one Species of Sugar, why should *France* be complimented with the Benefit of supplying *Europe* and herself
with

with that Species, which will amount to a prodigious Sum?

What I have said upon this Island is in all Respects applicable to *Hispaniola*.

But I own, it is not likely, that one Island should produce all the different Sorts of Sugars required. The *French* undoubtedly think so too. And therefore probably, they insist upon the Restitution of all. And if all is restored to them, they will be restored to the Enjoyment of the whole Sugar Trade, and in Consequence of it, of the *African* Trade likewise. Their Demand is certainly completely impudent. But who would not ask unreasonably, where he believes nothing that can be asked will be denied? O, with what Charitable, Compassionate and merciful *Samaritans*, doth *Great Britain* abound? and certainly blessed are the Peace Makers.

The *Havannah* is, as we are by the publick News Papers informed, to be restored to the *Spaniards* if it shall be taken.

Since it hath pleased God to bless the National Arms with Success against the *Havannah*, it will puzzle all the World, to find out a National Reason for restoring to the *Spaniard* after his unjust Declaration of War against us, attended with the most unwarrantable Circumstance of Insincerity and Treachery, the back Door to all his rich Possessions in *America*: especially after so much *British* Blood and Treasure Spent, as the taking that important Place hath cost us. But whoever reflects (I mean if the published and uncontradicted Preliminaries are true) on the exuberant and more than Christian Charity, Compassion and Mercy of our most charitable, compassionate and merciful *Samaritans* towards the *French*; he will soon divest himself of all Surprise, since he cannot but think, the *Spaniard* to the full as deserving as *France* of this *Samaritan* Tenderness.

But happy, thrice happy are our *Samaritans*, not only

only in a second Opportunity of exercising their charitable Dispositions; but also in that, which the Surrender of the *Havana b* hath furnished them, of demonstrating to the World, that as they far surpass the highly applauded Pattern of Charity in the Gospel, so they no less surpass in the *Glory* of *Heroism*, the earliest Warriors of Antiquity; who invaded their inoffensive Neighbours and spilt *their* Blood, and that of *their own* Subjects, with no other view, than of acquiring the Glory of Conquering: and, contented with Victory, restored their Conquests to the Invaded. But what transcending heroic Glory do the published Preliminaries promise, to our more than Christian Heroes and *Samaritans*, by informing us, that they are to restore to both our transgressing and injurious Enemies, whatever we have taken from them in Consequence of our necessary Defence?

My Lord and Sirs, I will now lay before you in one View, a Sketch of the Value of the Present, said to be intended, by our generous Conceders to be made to *France* only.

We are then humbly to crave of our defeated, routed, ruined, and first-aggressing Enemy, their favourable Acceptance of all their late Sugar Islands; the Products of which, when sold in foreign Markets, are worth to her upwards of 1,400,000*l.* Sterling *per Annum*, over and above her own Consumption, that cannot be estimated at less than 200,000*l.* which she must buy of us, when we take *Hispaniola*: in all 1,600,000*l.* And also the Right of Fishing for her home Consumption, which cannot be reckoned at so little as 500,000*l. per Annum*; all together 2,100,000*l.* with one Third at least, of the best Nursery for Seamen in the World; which they declare they will have to themselves, by desiring Stages and drying rooms to cure a Commodity unfit for her own Consumption, and only fit for the Markets she pretends to cede us. Besides this 2,100,000*l. per Ann.* we give her Grace, that yields up to her almost the whole *African* Trade: And Per-

dicherry, and two other Settlements in the *East Indies*, which, all together, cannot be much less than 1,000,000*l*. So that I dare say, according to the reported Preliminaries, we are to buy at the Price of near 3,000,000*l*. Sterling *per Annum*, a shameful and dishonourable Peace of vanquished *France*; in no Condition to take a single Foot of Land from us, but by Stealth, and through the Negligence of those, whose Office and Duty it is to prevent her: As in the Case of her late Descent upon *Newfoundland*, for which *some* Body deserves to be severely punished.

These are not all the Disadvantages of the promulged Preliminaries; for if, by Means of the Privilege of erecting Stages and drying Rooms on the Islands of *Newfoundland* and *Cape Sable*, the *French* should recover of the Fish Trade, what they pretend to give up, they will gain near 800,000*l*. more; which may fairly be added to the above Sum, as they will certainly regain it. Besides, as the last-mentioned Island is situated in the Center of the *New England* Fishery, (for it is well known the *New Englandmen* catch most of their Baccalea on *Sable* Bank) and very near the Track of the Ships bound to *Boston* and the other Ports of *New England*, *France* will doubtless make Forts and Settlements on the last-mentioned Island for the Security of her Ships of Force, with which she will most certainly, at some future Time, endeavour to ruin the *New England* Fishery, and intercept her Trade: To prevent which, to protect our *Newfoundland* Fishery, and to watch their Ships in their Voyage back to *Europe*, we must be at the constant Expence of keeping a large Squadron of Men of War in those Seas.

We can never be secure from an Intercourse between our future M———rs and those of H———r; who, if the former are to be corrupted, will scarce let them want a Temptation, to betray their Country. His Majesty hath indeed been pleased most graciously to assure us from the Throne, that his " Heart is intirely

tirely *British*", and it is surely utterly impossible, that his Majesty's religious and pious Disposition, will suffer him to deviate the least Jota from Sincerity and Truth. What a Thunder-bolt is this to fall in *H———r!* which hath, for near half a Century, been reaping the Fruits of *British* Industry and Toil, draining us of our Treasure, and spilling our Blood to aggrandize herself—and thereby giving the *French* favourable Opportunities of stealing our Trade, and raising terrible Fleets, that would have inevitably destroyed this Country, if *Gallic* Alertness, and Impatience to extinguish our Name and Nation, could have waited twenty Years longer, till the farther Reduction of our Commerce had rendered our naval Force too impotent to have prevented our intire Ruin! Therefore, though his " Majesty's Heart is intirely *British*," we cannot imagine, that those of the *H———r-M———rs* can be so—they are Natives of *H———r*, not of *Britain*. Happy would it be for us, if we could at any Time say, that the Hearts of our *M———rs* are like his Majesty's. But as this Blessing, if we may judge from past Experience, is not to be expected; we may reasonably apprehend, that the *M———rs* of the Electorate will not *sparingly* scatter our *own* Specie amongst those of *Great Britain*, in order to secure that System of continental Politics, the Advantages of which they only have reaped. I say our *own* Specie, for I believe three Score Years ago, they had none of their own. And if the *French* should have swept their Coffers clean, and reduced them to their original Indigence,——rather than not keep their old Pocket-Pistol in Repair, ready to point at our Breasts if we should presume to object to their stealing our Baccaloa, or to any other Breach of so *fine* a Treaty, they doubtless will begrudge no necessary Expence.

So then, according to the uncontradicted Preliminaries published, we are to pay *France* down in Hand 3,000,000*l*.

3,000,000*l.* Sterling *per Annum* for a Peace, with the Means of acquiring near a 1,000,000*l.* more in the Fishery; which will put her in Possession again of the same greater Share of that prodigious Nursery of Seamen, and divesting us of the whole in Time;—and likewise the Means of depriving us of the *Portugal* Trade, which has ever been estimated at 1,000,000*l.* Sterling *per Annum.*——For whenever an Intercourse is settled between the *British* and Electoral M——ries, if *France* with *Spain* should attack *Portugal*, we, however obliged by Treaty or Interest, must not dare to assist her (if able) for Fear—of exposing H——r to the Resentment of *France.*——O may the heaviest Vengeance in the Stores of Heaven, pursue them who shall contribute but a single Mite to the Destruction of my Country! O *Britain*, what will four or five Millions gain upon thy Commerce avail thee, if thy M——rs should ever spend six Millions annually in *Germany*, upon a *German* System? Will not the World view thee in the same ridiculous Light it doth the unwary Prodigal, that suffers himself to become the Bubble of some common Sharper, who, not worth a Groat, preys upon the giddy Fool of Fortune?

But one C——t Advocate will tell you, that *Great Britain* must preserve the Ballance of Power in *Europe.*——What, can she preserve that Ballance by running out her whole Estate, beggaring herself, and becoming a Bankrupt? Can a Spend-thrift, Beggar, and Bankrupt, be a Mediator in private Disputes, and a Composer of Quarrels in private Families? No more can a beggared and bankrupt Nation be a Mediator between jarring States, and Composer of Differences, or hold the Ballance of Power.

Another will tell you, that we are bound in Gratitude to preserve the King's *German* Dominions; for that they are endangered by our *American* Quarrel with *France.* I own I do not easily conceive, how one State can draw upon itself the Resentment of

another

another at War, unless she becomes a Party in the War, or assists in some Shape the Power with which it is at War. In both these Cases the Electorate is certainly innocent, with Regard to *Britain*. Her Situation and her Interest is confined to the Continent. —Our Situation is in the Ocean, and our Interest is in a Commerce extended over the whole World; wherein she can have no Right nor any Share, unless her Advocates will own that she sucks most of the Fruits of our Merchant's Labours. And as to any Assistance she has given us—I never heard that we owe her any Thanks upon that Account. Indeed she once sent us some Troops, (who had the Insolence to refuse Obedience to our Laws) when we had no Manner of Need of them; by which she affronted the Nation, as it implied a strong and groundless Suspicion of our Loyalty and Courage: And for the *no* Service of them we paid her a very large Sum of Money, which might have been much better employed, and which I heartily wish we had kept amongst ourselves; though we have paid immense Sums to the *Hessians*, and other petty States, to cover the Electorate in those Dangers to which the Ambition of her M――rs exposed her.

Her aspiring Views, some People have been free enough to think, have at several Times been the Occasion of the Variety of those contradictory Treaties, that have been attended with unsupportable Expences to this Country; and have manifested such an incurable Love in *certain* Persons, that discovered a fatal Secret to *France*; which was, that her threatening the Electorate, would strike such a Terror into some Natives of this Island, as would induce them to permit her to play what Pranks she pleased in *America* or elsewhere. If this be so—then it seems pretty clear, that all the Dangers which either the Electorate or *Great Britain* has lately known, are to be laid to the Door of that *German* Province only; that *A-*

American Quarrel is the Consequence of her aspiring Views; and that her Misfortunes are not the Consequences of our *American* Quarrel. And, as nothing can, I think, be more evident than this, so nothing can more forcibly prove, the absolute Expediency of a national Application to Parliament, to take into Consideration the proper Methods, of obtaining a total Seperation of that Electorate from *Great Britain*; to recal the *British* Troops from *Germany*, put a final Stop to continental Measures, and to turn our whole Strength against *France* and *Spain* in *America* and upon the Sea; and not to sheath the Sword before *France* is driven intirely out of it.

My Lord and Sirs, having laid before you the several Preliminaries, communicated to the Public by the News Papers, with the fatal Consequences to this Country, (should they be carried into Execution,)— together with such Observations upon them, as have occurred to me; it may not be amiss to ask, a few Questions, to which, I believe the Nation is curious enough to desire distinct Answers;

Whether any Nation can have a Right to invade another, or any of its Colonies and Possessions, and to butcher the People without Mercy, either by themselves or by inhuman Savages?

If any Nation is so unjustly invaded and injured, has she not a Right, by the Law of Nature, the Law of Nations, and the Law of God, to defend herself against such an Enemy and make Reprisals, to keep what she takes in War to indemnify herself for all the Charges of a War entered upon in her just Defence, and to distress the Aggressor so far as is necessary for her own future Security and Peace?

Hath not *France*, without the least Provocation from us, invaded and plundered our Colonies and Possessions in *America*, in Breach of Treaties, and inhumanly butchered our Fellow-Subjects, both by themselves and *Indian* Savages?

Hath

Hath not *Great Britain* the same Right in common with all Nations to defend herself against such Injuries done her by *France*, and to retain what she has taken from her in the present just and necessary War, in order to indemnify herself for the Charges of it, and establish her future Security and Peace?

Can *Great Britain* restore any of her Conquests in *America* or *Africa* to *France*, without restoring to her the Power of endangering her Security and Peace, but also of putting a total Period to her national Existence?

Hath not *France* been a most notorious Treaty Breaker, and hath she not broke every Treaty she ever made with this Nation?

Can *Great Britain*, consistent with her own Security and Peace, or any Rule of Policy, trust that notorious Treaty breaking and perfidious Nation?

Is any one Concession made by *France*, in the Preliminaries published, that can possibly indemnify *Great Britain* for the immense Charges she has been at in defending her just Rights and protecting her Subjects from *French* Violences, and herself from *French* Slavery; and why is so material and necessary an Article omitted in the Preliminaries?

Can our more than Christian *Samaritans* and most illustrious Heroes, since the Days of the first Warriors, whose Examples they seem so closely to imitate, produce a single Instance from History of any Nation, that, after being in a less Degree than we have been, unjustly invaded and injuriously treated, restored their Conquests to the offending Party, if she herself was in a Condition to maintain them; especially when such a Restitution would have enabled her Enemy to have completed her Ruin; and are not we in a Condition to maintain our Conquests over *France*, and to secure ourselves for the future against the fatal Effects of her boundless Ambition; and must we not expect all the Calamities of a conquered People, if we again

again truft her with thofe Weapons which will impower her to work our Deftruction, and which we are fure fhe will employ to that purpofe?

What National Reafon can be given for making Conceffions to conquered *France* that fo evidently tend to her Exaltation and the Perdition of *Great Britain?*

Is it poffible for any *Briton* in the South or North of this Ifland, to approve of Conditions fo fhameful, difhonourable, injurious, and fatal to his Native Country?

If any fuch there fhould unhappily be, will he not juftly deferve that fevere Juftice which is due to the higheft Crimes it is poffible to commit; and if a punifhment adequate to the Offence is unknown to our Laws, will not a Law *ex poft facto* be neceffary and warrantable, in order to prevent fuch dangerous Evils for the future, by ftriking a proper Terror into the Hearts of all future M———rs?

My Lord and Sirs, we have feen what generous and aftonifhing Conceffions, the Public Papers have made to *France*, and what niggardly and difadvantageous ones that artful and treacherous Court, hath made to us. The former I have largely treated, but I cannot difmifs you, without a Word or two upon the latter.

Surely then *France*, how deficient foever we take her to be, in the Point of Modefty, could never have the Impudence, to make fuch infolent Demands from *us*; and offer on her Part fuch mean Conceffions to *our* C—t. Therefore, if fuch Preliminaries are in Agitation, they muft be the fpontaneous Offers of our modern *Samaritans* and Heroes; who difdain to be out-done in Charity or Glory by thofe of Antiquity.

For all the rich and fertile Sugar Plantations, worth 1,400,000 fterling *per Annum*, conquered, ruined *France* is gracioufly pleafed to relinquifh to *Great Britain*, *Tobago* and the reft of the neutral Iflands, which would coft her incredible Sums to fettle; and which,

if

if settled, would be of no Use to her, since *France*, by underselling her, would enjoy the foreign Markets.

For *Goree*, which, for the Reasons already assigned, will not only put *France* in Possession, in a Manner, of the whole Trade of *Africa*, and that of *New Spain*, but also of a Situation, from whence she may dislodge us: She humbly condescends to permit *Great Britain* to retain *Senegal*, that, without *Goree*, will be useless to her.

For an immediate Right to at least One-third of the *Newfoundland* Fishery, under the Pretence of supplying her Home Consumption, which is worth between 5 and 600,000*l*. Sterling *per Annum*, and for the Liberty of erecting Stages, in order to engross the whole Fish Trade, besides the much more useful Privilege of nursing up immediately 16,400 Seamen —and the Opportunity of raising in Time 30,096 Seamen, the Number she had before the last War. For these Advantages, I say, *France* is willing to give up *Canada* and *Lousiana*; neither of which she can keep, if we otherwise please; and which is thinly peopled and scarce cultivated, and to and from whence six or ten Ships, at most, are employed. A mighty Concession this indeed! and such as a wise and honest M——ry would have rejected with the utmost Disdain.

If all the *Quid-Nuncs* of the Earth can produce an Instance of any Nation that, after receiving such audacious Affronts and Injuries as we have received from *France*, and after having so gallantly defended herself and reduced the Transgressor to the lowest Condition, next to Extirpation, put herself, when a glorious Conqueror, into the State of the conquered, and submitted to such Terms of Peace as those exhibited, I will readily submit to undergo all the Punishments due to those, who are bold enough to sacrifice their Country in the most shameful and disgraceful Manner.

God be praised we are at this Day a conquering Nation.—The national Armaments commanded by the

the valiant Earl of *Albemarle* by Land, and the valiant Admiral *Pocock* by Sea, have given so effectual a Stab to the Pride of the deceitful *Spaniard*, by the Reduction of the *Havannah*, and the Capture of so many *Spanish* Men of War, that it clearly demonstrates the Facility of the last Blow, necessary to be given to the united Houses of *Bourbon*, by the Reduction of the Island of *Hispaniola*.

When this glorious Stroke is struck, we shall be in Possession of the whole Sugar Trade, and of the fore and back Doors of all *Spanish America*; which will be such a Curb to the King of *Spain*, as will render his Alliance with the *French* King of so little Service to him, that it will of Course dissolve that Union between them, which was lately alarming to *us*, and dangerous to all *Europe*.

Then it will be Time, and not before, to sheath the Sword drawn against the *Spanish* Monarch, and to make Peace with *Spain*. But the Time can never come, when it will be proper to sheath it against *France*, who will be strong enough still to disturb her Neighbours, who, in Point of Commerce, will be no stronger than herself; and whom it will always be our Interest and Glory to protect with our Fleets, against her Injustice, Pride, and Insolence: Over her false and iniquitous Head, the protecting and avenging Sword of Justice should ever hang unsheathed.—And what Native soever of *Great Britain* shall take it down, and lay it by to rust in its Scabbard, at least before the perfidious *French* are reduced to a total Incapacity of doing Mischief, that Native *will* deserve to fall by the *Ax* or the *Halter*.—A War against *France* by Sea, we still are, and always shall be, able to carry on, exhausted as we are; provided we shake off our Shoulders that intolerable Weight, that had well nigh crushed us to Death; and which, if we do not, *even* the *little* Duke of *Wolfenbuttle*, could he amass Money sufficient to fit out a *few* flat-bottom'd Boats,

to

to embark his *few* Troops, would, in Time, be a Match for *Great Britain*, that hath reduced formidable *France* almoſt to the mean Condition of a *German* Prince. Doth it not therefore greatly behove this Nation to recal her Troops from *Germany*, falling there by Sickneſs, Fire, and Sword, in continental Broils, attended with an Expence of 6,000,000*l.* Sterling *per Annum*, when, if we retain all our Conqueſts, we ſhall not receive, upon the Ballance of our Trade, above 4 or 5,000,000*l.* ? And if we cannot proceed in the continental Syſtem, without running continually in Debt, how ſhall we be able to bear up againſt the Burthen, if we reſtore to *France* at once three Millions out of that four or five, with a Chance of ſoon worming us out of the Remainder; a Chance, attended with ſuch a fair Proſpect of Succeſs, that, but to call it a Chance, carries the Appearance of a down-right Abſurdity ?

Can then *any* Thing induce our Rivals of the charitable and merciful *Samaritan*, and of the generous Warriors of the earlieſt Ages, to pick the Pockets of their own Countrymen of three, perhaps five Millions Sterling *per Annum*; and thereby ſtarve all the Merchants, Manufacturers, Artificers, Shop-keepers, Seamen, Freeholders, Farmers, and Day-Labourers, together with all the Nobility and Gentry of this united Kingdom; and deſtroy the Navy of *Britain*, only to enrich and aggrandize *France*; the implacable Enemy of this Nation? No ſurely.—Nor can they have any national Reaſon for it : And if not, what Reaſon—or rather—what Motive can they have, to prompt them to a Meaſure pregnant with inevitable Perdition to their Country ?

When, with the unanimous Voices of this (in ſuch a Caſe) greatly injured Nation, they ſhall ſtand at the awful Tribunal of the Houſe of Lords, impeached by the Commons of *Great Britain*; will they plead in their Defence, that the Charms of Power and large Salaries

Salaries were so bewitching and irresistible, and their Abilities so inadequate to the arduous Affairs of War, that if they had not made Peace, they could not have retained either Power or Places. Or will they take off the Mask and own, that receiving from the Ministry of H——r a most melancholy Relation of the distressed and deplorable Situation of the E———te, and her dreadful Apprehensions of another Visit from the *French* Troops, their tender Hearts melting, could not bear her Sufferings. That sensible of the national Inabilities to continue the War in *Germany*, and, at the same Time, to defend our Conquests in *America*, and of their own Inabilities to carry on any War at all, they preferred a Peace with *France* upon any Conditions, to the sad Necessity of exposing H——r, and of resigning their Power and Employments.

Such Pleas—let them make if they durst: Neither will avail them; for if the last is their Motive, it will fix the Argument upon a certain Point. For is it fitting, that this great, populous, and commercial Nation, that raised the H——se of H——r to the Imperial Throne of these Realms, to secure all her Rights and Privileges, and to promote her Interest and Glory, should, contrary to the true Meaning and Spirit of the Act of Settlement, give to *France*, for the Security of H——r, the selfish Views of whose M——rs have drawn so many Misfortunes upon us, and exposed us to the greatest Dangers, three Millions Sterling *per Annum*, perhaps five Millions; together with the great Nursery of our naval Strength?——Upon this single Point then I rest the Argument. And do you yourselves then judge, whether, if this really or probably is the Case, an Application to the Legislature, to take proper Measures to obtain a total Separation of the *German* Dominions will not be absolutely necessary, for the future Security of this Island.

Do

Do not my dear and worthy old Friends and Masters, yet despair, tho' you should hear *French* Gold Chink, and *French* Chains and Fetters rattle all around you.——God hath often, very often in a most unexpected and wonderful Manner, delivered *Old England*, threatened with Destruction, from the wicked Machinations of evil Councellors and foreign Enemies.

Let *Englishmen* and all *Britons* then trust in God, their hitherto constant Protector; and let them not be wanting to themselves in an inactive and fruitless Despondency.——A proper Exertion of the legal and constitutional Weapons, which his good Providence, and the Virtues of our Fore-fathers have put in our Hands, may, and I doubt not will still save this sinking Land.

Besides, the Act of Settlement, which is a particular Compact between *Great Britain* and the House of *H———r*; we have the Bill of Rights which is a Renewal of the ancient, original, *Saxon* Compact between *Old England* and her Kings, confirmed and enforced thereby. This powerful Weapon, in the Hands of free-born *Britons*, hath removed all Obstacles in the Peoples Way to the Throne; and gives them an Approach to the Royal Ear.——So that if they are not negligent of their own Interest, and Happiness, and willing to be undone, they may lay all their Greivances before their Princes, represent the State of Things and the Misconduct of Ministers, and pray for Redress and for the Removal of Evil Councellors.

The Doors of both Houses of Parliament also are, from the Nature of our happy Constitution, ever open to the Petitions of the People. and the Ears of the Members ever attentive to their Complaints: and whenever the People think fit to apply to them for Redress of Grievances, or the Punishment of evil Councellors, there can be no Doubt, but their Applications will be favourably received, and their Expectations fully satisfied;—even, tho' through a Deficiency of the Laws or Artifices used to evade the force of them, Delinquents may be so protected from adequate Punishments, that the People may be driven to the Necessity of praying for a Law *ex post Facto*, to reach them.

An humble and early Approach to the Throne, may often prevent national Misfortunes, especially such as are likely to happen in the Intervals of the Parliaments Sittings, when it is impossible to apply to their own Representatives, and implore the Protection of either House of Parliament. Whether the present Crisis is a seasonable Time for the Exertion of such Rights and Privileges you yourselves are the best Judges.

I have, my Lord and Sirs, gone through all the Preliminaries of a Peace, which the hitherto uncontradicted News Papers, have been pleased to alarm the Nation with; except that, which relates to the exchange of *Minorca* for *Belleisle*.——I believe you will not think it necessary, to say any thing more upon this Head, than, that if the other Preliminaries are true, both these Places will be equally useless to us, since we shall soon have neither Commerce nor Fleets.

And now, my Lord and Sirs, I dare say you will think it full Time to release you, and lay down my Pen. But yet I crave your Patience for a short Word more.

Nothing, believe me, could have engaged me in this long Task but my Love to my Country, and my Love and Gratitude to the City of *London*, whose Dangers I see in the Light I have set them in to the Public. In these Sheets I have delivered nothing but what I really believe to be Fact, or any Sentiment, but what exactly corresponds with my Heart. And in laying these things before you and my Country, I have not, nor can have any other View, than the Good and Prosperity of my Fellow-Citizens and Fellowlow-Subjects. I flatter myself with a full Persuasion, that you think I served you, in the Vigour of my Life faithfully, honestly, and with the Spirit of an *Englishman*, however unqualified I might be in the Point of Abilities, to serve you as I wished. If therefore I am not mistaken in this Persuasion, I may reasonably hope, for the Continuance of your former Confidence in your *Old* Servant, now I am far advanced in Years, and arrived at a Time of Life, when I ought daily to expect my call hence. And certainly it is now much too late to turn Villain, when I see *Old Time* aiming his Scythe at me, and unrelenting Death looking me full in the Face, and pointing to my Tomb. These, believe me, my good and Worthy old Friends and Masters, are no frightful Spectres, nor unpleasant Reflections to your Old Servant, who at the same time that he indulges these Ideas, can lay his Hand upon his Heart, and say, with Truth, I never betray'd my Trust—nor sold my Country.—— May Almighty God deliver this Nation from her present Fears;——May true Religion and unsullied Virtue abound, and Liberty and Commerce flourish throughout this Island.——Parliaments remain uncorrupt, and Wisdom, Justice, and Goodness grace the Throne of these Realms;—and may the choicest Blessings in the Stores of Heaven, fall in plenteous Showers upon the City of *London* for evermore. These are my sincere and most hearty Wishes; and I pray God grant them.—Years render Travelling unpleasant: I shall scarce see my Old Constituents any more, and therefore I now take my last leave of you.—— May I hope that the present Inhabitants of *London* will, when I am laid in my Grave, remember they once had a Servant, who bore the Name of

GEORGE HEATHCOTE.

Farewel,— Farewel.

Hereford, October 6, 1762.

POST-

POSTSCRIPT.

N. B. Since I sent this Letter to the Press, I have been well informed, that all my Computations are much too low in Favour of *France*; particularly my Computation of 200,000*l. per Annum* for her Products of Indigo, Cotton, Coffee, Pimento, *&c.* are much too low; that they amount at least to 500,000*l. per Annum*, which makes the Profit arising to *France* 300,000*l. per Annum* more than I have made it. This Difference will turn in Favour of *France* the Ballance of 269,162 *l.* stated before in our Favour, upon a Supposition of restoring the *French* Sugar Islands, and permitting the *French* only to supply their Home Consumption of Fish, to which if we add the Value of the *African* Trade by the Restitution of *Goree*, and a Share of the *East India* Trade by that of *Pondicherry*, I verily believe the Ballance in Favour of *France* against *Great Britain* will not be much less than one Million Sterling, exclusive of a Ballance in Favour of the former upon the other Trade of *Europe*, which I fear is the Case. All these Trades must be esteemed so many Nurseries for Seamen, tending to the Advancement of the *French* naval Power, and when added to One-third of the *American* Fishery only, must furnish *France* with more Seamen than the Remainder of our Trade can do. *France* thus increasing both in Riches a Million more than *Great Britain per Annum*, and also proportionably in naval Power, can this Nation possibly long resist her Efforts to destroy her? If it cannot long resist—how soon must it become the Prey of *France*, when *France* has recovered the same Share of the Fishery she had before the War, which added, will put her in Possession of 3 or 4,000.000*l. per Annum*, whilst *Great Britain* will be reduced to her Tobacco, Rice, and small Remainder of the Fishery, all which together will not exceed
1,200,000*l.*

1,200,000*l. per Annum?* Let our wife Politicians ponder thefe Things, and tremble.

Although I could have enhanced the prefent, faid to be intended for the favourable Acceptance of our ever perfidious Enemy fome Millions, I chufe rather that the Judgments of Mankind fhould be at prefent formed upon the very moderate Computation in the foregoing Letter, as that is fufficient to prove the intire Deftruction of this Country, if a Peace fhould be concluded upon the Preliminaries reported; efpecially as the Merchants, if they pleafe to ftate fuch an Account as I have taken the Liberty to recommend, will do it with an Exactnefs, that the Friends of *France* and H——r will not be able to contradict it.

I chofe to treat the Subject of the Fifhery in the preceding Pages, upon the latter Report fpread that the *French* were only to fifh for their Home Confumption, as the moft favourable to our excellent and wife Adminiftration, and, perhaps, given out by them to abate the Refentment of the Nation for the prefent. Remember, my old Friends and Mafters, that no Nation can poffibly exift long when it relaxes Juftice, which you need not fear to obtain, through the Vigilance and Integrity of a *Britifh* Parliament; and fhould you ever have Occafion to bring Minifters to Juftice whilft Mr. *Pitt* lives—let me recommend to you fuch a Confidence in that true Patriot, as will prevent all Sufpicion of his Fidelity. If he fhould judge it proper to form any Connections with old Offenders—that poffibly may be a very neceffary Step—whom, if they heartily concur in bringing new Ones to Juftice, I hope, upon fuch Conditions, and upon fuch Conditions only, you will forgive and forget their paft Faults.

Hereford, Oct. 16, 1762.

APPENDIX.

The British Merchant, *from* P. 284 *to* P. 296. *Vol.* II.

BUT that I may not be misunderstood, as if I were pleading for the *Dutch*; for whereinsoever they are our Rivals in Trade, they are to be guarded against. But I am shewing, we ought to be more jealous of the *French*, who are more our Rivals in Trade. And, in order to do this, I shall shew the *Mercator*'s Partiality, by representing truly the State of the *French* Trade; and adding to the *Mercator*'s two Instances several others, wherein the *French* are our Rivals, at least equally, if not in a greater Degree, than the *Dutch* are.

He has omitted to charge to the Account of the *French* their rivalling us in the Fishery. He charges this to the Account of the *Dutch*; and tells us very truly, that they are increased in the Herring Fishery; I hope he will not say, in Red Herrings; that, he knows, is not true: For they make none but White Herrings. They catch them in the open Sea, near the Coast of *Scotland*; and carry them to *Holland*, and prepare them. Their Industry in this is to be commended; and the Supineness and Negligence of the *Scotch* and *English* to be blamed; not that they do not hinder them, but that they do not imitate their Industry and Vigilance. He says, they used to pay an Acknowledgment for this: I wish they did so still. But I shall tell him presently of another Nation, that paid a Duty for catching Fish; which has been long since discontinued, through the Faults of some Persons formerly; and that they are now very far from being again reduced to a Condition, of being ever forced to renew the Payment of that Duty. He says,
the

the *Dutch* have beaten us out of the Whale Fishing. He has forgot, that the *French* have a very great Fishery of that Kind; but it did not serve his Purpose, to say any Thing of the *French* White Fishery: That would have made against his good Friends; and therefore was to be passed over in Silence. Notwithstanding, the *French* Fishermen of *St. John de Luze, Bayonne*, and other Ports in that Part of the Bay of *Biscay*, are the most expert Harpooners in the World, without excepting the *Dutch* and *Hamburghers*. Whether the *Mercator* knew this or no, the *French* know it; and therefore took Care, by the late Treaty of Commerce, to have the Produce of Whales excepted, (not against us, says the *Mercator*, but) against the *Dutch*. 'Tis a Sign they think their own Fishery sufficient, at least, to supply themselves with the Produce of Whales, without being beholden either to the *Dutch* or *English*. The *Dutch* then are not the only Nation, that have wormed us out of this Trade; the *French* have done it too, to the vast Increase of their Navigation and Seamen.——

But the *French* have not only increased in the Whale Fishery, but, which is of much more Consequence to us, they have exceedingly increased their Fishery to *Newfoundland*, as well on the Coast, as on the great Bank. The Consequences of this Increase of their Fishery, we have, to our Sorrow, too sensibly felt; and yet they have found Advocates for it, who are ready to answer, when any Thing is represented against granting the *French* any Liberty of Fishery, What! must the *French* have nothing? So very kind are some Persons to them, that they are angry with their Fellow-Subjects, for endeavouring to exclude them that Fishery. The *French* do not only fish on the great Banks of *Newfoundland* for such Fish as is cured without drying, as the *Dutch* do in their White Herring Fishery in the open Sea; but have had the Address to obtain, that the Island of *Cape Breton* should

should be yielded up to them, to fortify and do what they please with: Where they may, and doubtless will, make another *Dunkirk*; and where they may carry on their dry Fishery, as well as at *Placentia*. We have an Account, that they have some Time ago sent Men of War to fortify *Cape Breton*; but, as if this was not Privilege enough for them, they have obtained, that, in the fishing Season, they may resort to the very Island of *Newfoundland* itself, and erect Stages, *&c* to cure and dry their Fish at. 'Tis a Sign they think this Liberty sufficient for them; for they have excepted against all this Sort of Fish, but what shall be in Barrels, by the late Treaty of Commerce. The *Mercator* cannot be so ignorant, as to suppose *Newfoundland* Fish, and especially the dry Fish, can be carried to *France* in Barrels, but at such an Increase of the Cost, as shall render the Sale impracticable in that Country, though the Duties there are sufficient to do this.

But this is not all; the World is well amended with the *French*, since the Time that they paid a Tribute for the Liberty of curing and drying Fish at *Newfoundland*; which was granted to them by King *Charles* the First, in the tenth Year of his Reign. At this present the *French* do not only pay no Tribute, but, by their Neighbourhood at *Cape Breton*, will oblige us to keep large Garrisons at *Newfoundland*, if we will prevent our being surprized there; where they will have the Liberty of the fishing Season, equally with us, from Cape *Bonavista* northward to the northern Point of the said Island, *&c.* by which Situation they will be our Rivals in another Branch of our Fishery, that of Salmon. For at the Harbour of *Bonavista*, which is to the Northward of the Cape, and therefore within their Limits, is an extraordinary good Fishery of Salmon. But this some wise Folks knew nothing of. Had the late King *William* granted the *Dutch* any one of the Islands of the *Orkneys*, in Propriety,

Propriety, to fortify; or a Liberty of restoring to, or of erecting drying Houses necessary to cure Red Herrings in any such Island, or in *England* or *Scotland*, it would have been remembered, with very good Reason, a thousand and a thousand Times over. So the *Mercator* may observe here, the *Dutch* nor *French* do neither of them pay the Duty they used to pay; but the *French* have had the Cunning to procure for their Fishery, such Liberties and Privileges as can scarcely be consistent with our Safety or Interest; and which the *Dutch* could not obtain from those, whom the *Mercator* counts their Friends. I leave the World now to judge, who are our *greatest* and *most dangerous* Rivals in the Fishery.

Not that I am so much concerned, that they do not now pay that Acknowledgment they formerly paid for the Liberty of fishing on the Island of *Newfoundland*, as I am, that they at any Time paid any such Acknowledgment: For certainly, without the Shadow of that Submission, they would not have been indulged in a Matter, that might, in its Consequence, prove as fatal to our Safety, as detrimental to our Commerce: And I cannot but think, that, notwithstanding the Interest the *French* had in the Court of *England*, by Means of the *French* Match they would hardly without this seeming Advantage, have obtained Leave to cure and dry their Fish upon the very Island of *Newfoundland* itself, whatever Leave might have been granted them of fishing upon the great Banks thereof; which are as much the Dependencies of that Island, as the Coasts and Banks, where the *Dutch* fish for Herrings off *Scotland*, and the North Parts of *England*, are belonging to *Great Britain*; and for which there was the same Reason to insist on a Duty to be paid by the *French*, though they should never set their Foot upon the Island, as there was for demanding it of the *Dutch* for what they caught here in the open Sea.—Every Body must acknowledge, that it was extremely the Interest of *France*, to submit to pay five *per Cent.* upon all the Fish, they caught and dryed at *Newfoundland*; that they might secure to themselves the Advantage of such a Nursery of Seamen.

They are now so much our Rivals in this Trade, and are increased to such a prodigious Degree, that they employ yearly from *St. Malo, Granville, Rochelle, St. Martins,* Isle of *Rea, Bayonne, St. Jean de Luze Sibour, &c.* to carry on their Fishery on the Great Banks of *Newfoundland,* and on the Coasts of that Island; that is, in their Wet and Dry Fish, upwards of four hundred Sail of Ships; They do not only now supply themselves with the Fish, they formerly had from us; but furnish many parts of *Spain,* and *Italy* therewith; and rival us there to our prodigious Loss. They have the properest Sort of Salt of their own, which renders their Voyages much shorter than ours. For we are oblig'd to go from hence to *Rochelle, Olleron, St. Martins, &c.* to fetch that Commodity, which they have at their own Doors; and thereby we most frequently spend a Month or six Weeks more in our Voyages than they do.

They are so extremely sensible of the prodigious Advantage of this Fishery, and so very intent upon pursuing it, that from their first Attempts to make themselves considerable at Sea, they have had it perpetually in View.—They first obtained leave to fish upon paying a Duty of 5 *per Cent.* afterwards they got that Acknowledgement relinquished: But they have lately gone much further: for in the present Treaty they have procured a Cession to be made to them of the Island of *Cape Breton,* a maiden Fishery, that has scarce ever been touched: whereas *Newfoundland* is almost exhausted, and also several Islands in the Gulph of *St. Laurence:* And not content with that, they have further obtained a Liberty of curing and drying their Fish; setting up Stages; and resorting to OUR
Island

Island of *Newfoundland*, during all the Time that it is of any Use to resort thither; that is, during the Fishing Season. They are, indeed, to deliver us up the Possession of *Placentia*, and some other places in *Newfoundland*: but then they have taken care to have a better Place yielded to them, in lieu thereof; with this extraordinary Favour to them more than to us, that they have the Liberty granted them to frequent Our Island of *Newfoundland*, and erect Stages, &c. thereon, for curing and drying their Fish: but we have not the Privilege allowed us of doing the same on any of their Islands, or on the Island of *Cape Breton*; which they have express Permission granted them to fortify as they please. Thus they are our Rivals in the FISHERY by our own Consent; which is the more wonderful, in that it is owing to this Fishery, that they dared to contend for the Mastery at Sea with the Maritime Strength of *England* and *Holland* united. 'Tis true, the *English* and *Dutch* are most frequently called the Maritime Powers; but I think it a Jest to appropriate the Name of Maritime Powers to *Great Britain* and *Holland*, exclusive of *France*, when we consider what a Figure that Nation made at Sea, before the Battle of *La Hogue* in 1692. Can we then think, that a few Years of Peace, with such a Fishery, and such Conditions of Commerce, as were to be granted to *France* by the late Treaty, will not then enable her to contend again with our united Fleets? The History, both of *France* and *England*, will shew you, that it is since their procuring Leave to fish at *Newfoundland*, that they have grown so formidable at Sea; and that their Navy Royal has augmented, in Proportion to the Numbers of Ships employed in that Fishery.—What have we not to expect then from them, now they have obtained a Right to a better Place for their Fishery, in the Opinion even of the *French* themselves, as you will see by the inclosed Letter, written by a Minister of State in *France* to

the

the Duke *de Gramond* at ayonne; and which I believe is Genuine. The Occasion of it was, that the People of *St. Jean de Luze* and *Sibour* (two places in the County of *La Bour*) being under Apprehensions that their Fishery at *Newfoundland* was to be delivered up wholly to us, the Duke wrote a Letter to *Paris* to be rightly informed; and received the following Answer.

Copy of a Letter written by Monsieur de Ponchartrain *to Monsieur the Duke* de Gramond, *from* Fontainbleau, 19 September, 1713.

"I Have received, Sir, the Letter you did me the Honour to write me the third of this Month, with two Letters that were directed to You by the Inhabitants of *St. Jean de Luze* and *Sibour*, upon the Subject of their Fishery of Dry Fish. From the Account I have given the King of their Demand, his Majesty directed me to write, by his Order to Monseigneur the Duke *d'Aumont*, his Ambassador Extraordinary at *London*, to ask of the Queen of *Great Britain* a Permission for them to go the next Year to *Placentia*; and the Liberty to continue their Fishery in ALL the Ports and Harbours upon the Coast of *Newfoundland*. I shall give myself the Honour to acquaint you with Monseigneur the Duke *d'Aumont*'s Answer. I agree with You, Sir, that the Country of *la Bour* will suffer very much, should they be deprived of their Liberty of carrying on their Fishery of Dry Fish; And you will be persuaded of the Attention I have to procure to the Merchants, that drive this Commerce, the Means *to continue them in it,* when I have informed you, that the King sent from *Rochford,* in the Month of *May* last, one Frigate to go and lay the first Foundation of an Establishment in the Island of Cape *Breton*; where Fish is MUCH MORE ABUNDANT, than at the Island of *Newfoundland*;

" *foundland*; and where one may *make the Fish, and*
" *manage the drying thereof easily*. This Frigate ar-
" rived *June* 26 at *Placentia*, from whence she was
" to continue her Course for *Cape Breton*; to which
" Place I have caused to be transported 100 Men,
" to begin the Settlement. His Majesty will send,
" in the Beginning of the Year, three Ships to trans-
" port thither the Garrison of *Placentia*, and the In-
" habitants of the Island of *Newfoundland*; and to put
" the last Hand to the Establishment of that Port.
" The Merchants of this Kingdom may then send
" all such Ships as they shall think fit to order for
" the fishing of dry Fish, and for the Oils that are
" made from the Fish on the said Island. This Fa-
" vour ought to animate the Merchants that drive
" this Commerce, to carry it on with Vigour, from
" the Advantage they will draw from it. This is all
" I have been able to do in their Favour. I desire
" you to be persuaded of the great Sincerity where-
" with I have the Honour to be——."

From this Letter, 'tis plain the *French* never intended to quit the Fishery of dry Cod; and that they have very much at Heart the rivalling us therein.

That, to secure themselves against any Accident, they were careful to send a Man of War in the Month of *May*, 1713, which was within a little Time after the signing the Treaty the 11th of *April* before, and had sent 100 Men to lay the first Foundations of their Fortifications at *Cape Breton*; and further assure the Duke, that three other Ships should be sent the Beginning of this Year, to transport the Garrison of *Placentia* thither, and put the last Hand to the Establishment of that Port; which, no Doubt, they will effect, before they deliver up *Placentia*: Not much unlike what they are doing under our Noses, making a *new* Port at *Mardyke*, before they fill up the *old* one at *Dunkirk*.

Another

Another Thing obfervable from this Letter is, that the *French* are *now fo fanguine* as not to content themfelves with the Ceffion of *Cape Breton*, and other Iflands thereabouts; or with the Liberty of erecting Stages, &c. to cure and dry their Fifh, from Cape *Bonavifta* Northward, and fo on to *Point Riche*, on the weftern Side; but are afking new Favours, and demand a Permiffion to *Placentia* this Year, (although the Time agreed for delivering that Place has been long fince expired) and fue for a Liberty to make their Fifh in all the Ports and Harbours upon the Coafts of *Newfoundland*: Which, though I make no Doubt but was denied them; yet I am amazed, that it fhould ever enter into their Heads, fo much as to attempt. Sure they think we can deny them nothing!

F I N I S.

www.ingramcontent.com/pod-product-compliance
Lightning Source LLC
Chambersburg PA
CBHW020729100426
42735CB00038B/1107